DEATH OF HOMETOWN

Yongtao Du

DEATH OF HOMETOWN

Political Elites and the Fate of Native Place in Modern China

The Asian Studies Collection

Collection Editor

Dong Wang

First published in 2025 by Lived Places Publishing

All rights reserved. No part of this publication may be reproduced, stored in a retrieval system, or transmitted in any form or by any means, electronic, mechanical, photocopying, recording or otherwise, without prior permission in writing from the publisher.

No part of this book may be used or reproduced in any manner for the purpose of training artificial intelligence technologies or systems. In accordance with Article 4(3) of the Digital Single Market Directive 2019/790, Lived Places Publishing expressly reserves this work from the text and data mining exception.

The author and editor have made every effort to ensure the accuracy of information contained in this publication, but assume no responsibility for any errors, inaccuracies, inconsistencies and omissions. Likewise, every effort has been made to contact copyright holders. If any copyright material has been reproduced unwittingly and without permission the Publisher will gladly receive information enabling them to rectify any error or omission in subsequent editions.

Copyright © 2025 Lived Places Publishing

British Library Cataloguing in Publication Data
A CIP record for this book is available from the British Library

ISBN: 9781916985094 (pbk)
ISBN: 9781916985117 (ePDF)
ISBN: 9781916985100 (ePUB)

The right of Yongtao Du to be identified as the Author of this work has been asserted by them in accordance with the Copyright, Design and Patents Act 1988.

Cover design by Fiachra McCarthy
Book design by Rachel Trolove of Twin Trail Design
Typeset by Newgen Publishing UK

Lived Places Publishing
Long Island
New York 11789

www.livedplacespublishing.com

Abstract

Anyang was founded as a county when China became a unified empire in the third century BCE. For centuries, local gentry made the county their home, where they buried their ancestors and dwelled with their kinfolk. Talented sons might have careers in the larger world of the empire, but eventually it was Anyang that they returned to in search of rest. The twentieth century witnessed fundamental changes to this scenario. Political and intellectual revolutions shattered the life-world of China, and transformed the meanings of life and place in Anyang. Now its brightest sons all left without returning.

Key words

place, lineage, "all-under-heaven," Communism, nationalism, Confucianism, revolution, oracle bones, New Culture Movement, local identity

Contents

Learning objectives viii
Prologue ix
Chapter 1 The new world 1
Chapter 2 The nation 23
Chapter 3 The home place 51
Chapter 4 The death of hometown 73
Epilogue 99
Discussion Questions 121
Notes 122
Recommended Further Readings 125
Index 127

Learning objectives

- Understand key revolutions in twentieth-century China and their impact on society.
- Explore significant intellectual movements in modern China and their influences.
- Examine the organization and significance of traditional spatial structures in Chinese civilization.
- Analyze interactions and impacts between local identities, national policies, and global influences.

Prologue

1.

In our modern world, Anyang, a county in the North China Plain about 350 miles south of Beijing, is best known for the ruins of an ancient capital of one of China's earliest dynasties, located just a couple of miles from the county seat (Figure 1). For thousands of years, the Chinese referred to the original name of the capital, Yin, and called the ruins "Yinxu," which literally means the "Ruins of the Yin." Although the locals were aware of the ruins and occasionally mentioned them in their writings, they never considered them particularly significant. In a country with so many ancient capital ruins, the "ruins of the Yin" did not stand out. The Shang dynasty, which existed between the sixteenth and eleventh centuries BCE, was too distant in time, and except for a few sketchy references in ancient history books, little was known about it. Other dynasties that had their capitals near Anyang were more captivating, better known, and more relatable. The ruins of these dynasties, that is, the northern dynasties during the so-called Barbaric Conquest in the third through fifth centuries CE, were more frequently mentioned in writings by both locals and visitors.

However, this scenario changed rapidly in the early twentieth century. At the beginning of the century, Chinese civilization was in a state of disintegration after several decades of resistance to Western influence, which had begun in earnest in the mid-nineteenth

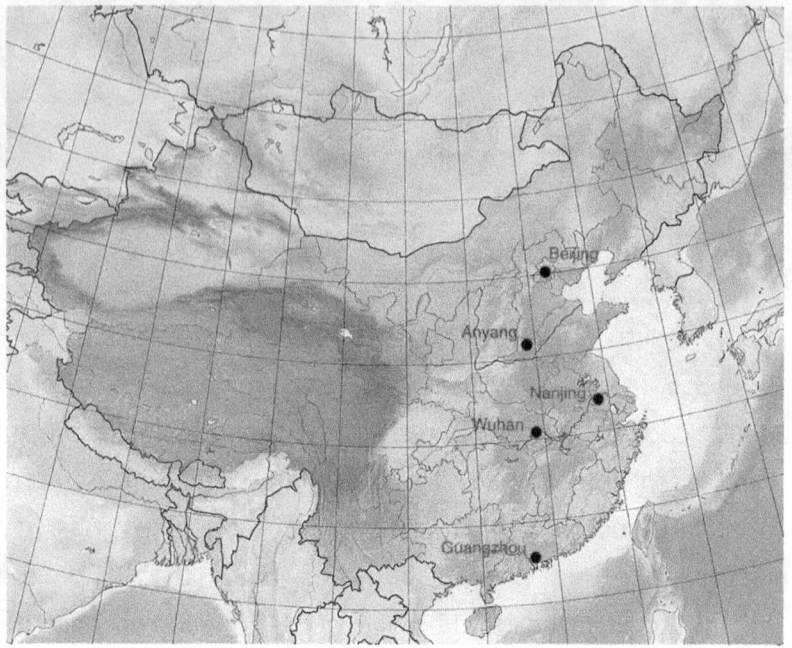

Figure 1 Anyang and other major cities in China

century. Alongside Western military and economic domination in the Far East came modern Western epistemological modes centered on scientism. In history writing and history teaching, this new outlook demanded empirical evidence as the foundation for historical knowledge, especially for periods the furthest back in time. Legendary ancient periods and figures, such as the sage kings and the states they founded, which had been accepted as real for centuries, were now scrutinized for their historicity. A new era of historical knowledge production and periodization had begun. The modern discipline of archaeology, which could most effectively test and verify the historicity of legends, was introduced and began to collaborate with traditional text-based scholarship to reorganize and reassess the country's ancient history.

The "Ruins of Yin" gained renewed significance under these circumstances. It became the location of China's first major archaeological excavation, conducted between 1928 and 1937, which unequivocally established the historicity of the Shang dynasty. However, comparable archaeological discoveries have not been made for legendary periods preceding the Shang, such as the Xia dynasty. As a result, the Shang became the earliest verified dynasty in Chinese history. The most important evidence unearthed from the site—the Oracle Bones, consisting of hundreds of thousands of turtle shells and cattle bones inscribed with texts—has also been recognized as the beginning of writing in China.

The excavations in Anyang, in terms of proving long-existing legends to be historical, can be compared to the remarkable work of the German amateur archaeologist Heinrich Schliemann, whose excavations in modern-day Turkey and Greece in the 1870s lent significant credibility to the idea that Homer's *Iliad* reflects historical events. Given this level of intellectual excitement, it is no wonder that Anyang soon gained fame as the site of China's most important archaeological discovery. The additional prestige of being the place where Chinese writing began, further enhanced Anyang's reputation, placing it among the privileged locations that can claim to be "the country's first" in some respect.

In 1977, Li Ji, the Harvard-trained founder of modern archaeology in China who directed the excavations in Anyang, wrote an account of his work there some 40 years earlier. This account, written in English and titled *Anyang*, became a modern classic and further consolidated Anyang's fame beyond China's borders.

All these factors—the intellectual excitement, the symbolic significance, and the international recognition—seemed to combine to create an unstoppable force that permanently associated Anyang with the archaeological site and its discoveries. By the end of the century, the two had become inseparable in writings about the area: Anyang is synonymous with the excavation site, and the site defines Anyang. Even when locals discussed Anyang among themselves, they would almost immediately bring up the topic of the excavation site.

Behind this branding, however, lies a deep irony for the place and its inhabitants. What the natives of a place truly need is a home—a place where they can dwell, live their lives, and perhaps even die their deaths. A dwelling place for mortal human beings is, as Martin Heidegger described it, a site they build in the world where they can "accept the heaven, preserve the earth, await the divine, and accompany the mortal."[1] An excavation site, no matter how important it may be in the professional world, has little to do with this essential need. For example, Li Ji's book, which took Anyang as its namesake, dedicated only two words to the place itself: "worth digging." The academic significance of the site and the other accolades it brought to Anyang are all about fame. But fame is not home.

The irony for the natives who loudly proclaim, "Anyang is the excavation site" is that, with each proclamation, and perhaps at the very moment of shouting, the true meaning of Anyang as their native place—their home where they could build a life—quietly recedes a little further. In fact, in the 1990s, when the branding of Anyang as an excavation site was gaining full momentum and becoming ubiquitous, China's intellectual culture was entering a period of profound anxiety often referred to by contemporaries as a "spiritual crisis." After the fervor of Communism had waned, and amid the rapid marketization of the economy and commercialization of society, educated people across the country, including the natives of Anyang, were gripped by a deep sense of angst—a feeling that they had lost the ground on which to "settle their being and establish meaning for life" (*anshen liming*).

An influential debate on this crisis within the Chinese intellectual scene lasted for several years, with many voices calling for the "reconstruction of a spiritual home." The differences and similarities between spiritual "homelessness" and the lack of a dwelling place on earth are likely too complex to fully explore here. However, it is clear that the widespread sense of homelessness in China toward the end of the century was related to, if not caused by, the way people talked about and engaged with their native places—exemplified by the natives of Anyang. If you do not view your native place (or, for that matter, any place where you reside) as a true place of dwelling, you will not have a place to call home. Fame, wealth, and all the other attributes one might ascribe to a place do not necessarily create a sense of home.

What happened to people of Anyang (and, more generally, to people of other places in China) during the twentieth century was that they lost their way of engaging with their native place as a place of home. To say they lost their way is to recognize that their predecessors (many of whom also their ancestors) who lived in the place knew and practiced it. As will be explained in more detail below, for centuries educated men in Anyang (as in other places of China) celebrated their native place primarily as their home: the place where they were born and raised, where their kinsmen lived and their ancestors were buried, where their careers began, and where they returned after journeys into the outside world.

These men were known as the literati (*shi*). Their career trajectory often followed a pattern: receiving schooling and preparing for the civil service examinations in their home place, moving on to provincial- and national-level examinations if they could pass the examinations at the local level, and eventually entering civil service and being posted in the capital or local places elsewhere. The outside world in which they operated was called the "all-under-heaven" (*tianxia*), a term commonly used to describe the territories encompassed by the universal state of China (known as the "Central Country") and, in any case, included most of the known world. In their self-perception, the literati saw themselves as gentlemen of the world, bearing noble obligations to lead the people and maintain order. Yet, they were also deeply rooted in their native places—places of beginning and ending. In fact, the "all-under-heaven" was essentially a collection of local places like their home. There was no need to brand the native place with anything extraordinary, although many naturally harbored pride in its distinctiveness and superiority over other places and often celebrated it in their writings. However, that kind of superiority and distinctiveness was defined within a framework of sameness: a place may be better in performing common moral duties or producing candidates in the same examination system, but all local places were building blocks of the "all-under-heaven" and could not be fundamentally different from one another.

That world of the "all-under-heaven" and its local places was the world of traditional Chinese civilization, sometimes called the Sino-centric world due to China's self-proclaimed centrality. This world collapsed in the twentieth century through confrontation and conflict with the modern West. The most direct consequence of this collapse was China's loss of centrality, and the Chinese state's loss of universal claims. This loss was keenly felt and painfully absorbed by Chinese intellectuals, the modern counterparts of the literati. However, this loss did not necessarily mean that modern Chinese would also lose their connection to their native places and a sense of rootedness there.

The loss of the ability to engage one's native place as a place of home, as seen in the natives of Anyang, was not an inevitable consequence of the beginning of modern times or the collapse of traditional Chinese civilization. One clear piece of evidence for this in Anyang is the 1933 edition of the county's local gazetteer. The local gazetteer is the periodically updated book of the local places that local elites had been engaged in compiling for centuries whereby they not only recorded the historical, geographical, financial, and other practical knowledge about their local places but also registered and celebrated their local identity. In this edition of the Anyang County gazetteer, local elites wrote about and celebrated their native place in much the same way as the literati had done for centuries. Although the excavations at the "Ruins of Yin" and the oracle bones they uncovered had already made headlines worldwide, the locals remained composed. Rather than branding the place with the excavation site, they treated the archaeological site and the oracle bones as parts of their heritage. The gazetteer included two appendices: one on stone inscriptions discovered in the Anyang region over the centuries, and another on the recently excavated oracle bone inscriptions. The connotation is subtle but revealing: despite the oracle bones' global impact, they were regarded as just another form of inscription in a place that had known such artifacts for centuries.

The loss of the ability to engage with the native place as a place of home—or simply put, the death of the hometown—must have occurred sometime after the gazetteer's compilation and must be explained by factors other than the collapse of China's centrality. This book argues that between the fall of traditional China at the beginning of the twentieth century and the rise of Communist China in the middle of the century, there were genuine opportunities for locally rooted people to recalibrate the relationship between home, country, and the world. They had the chance to reposition themselves in this emerging new world in a way that acknowledged the new world order while retaining their connection to their native place. What follows is the story of one man's efforts to do just that. In his failure, we may glimpse the fate of locality in modern China and gain a deeper understanding of the tragedy of those who became disconnected from their roots.

2.

The man's name is Zhang Jinjian. He was born in 1902, nine years before the collapse of the country's last dynasty—the Qing—and the founding of the Republic of China. His life witnessed not only the political but also the cultural turmoil that the country experienced during its migration into the modern world. First, the universal state collapsed, and then the orthodox learning—often conveniently called Confucianism—that had buttressed the state and the social-moral order of China during the past centuries went bankrupt and was replaced by a set of new and competing ideas and ideologies imported from the West. The decade or so between the mid-1910s and mid-1920s in China is often labeled the "New Culture Movement" because of these new ideas that swept the country's cultural and intellectual scene. The new generation of youth that was shaped by the new cultures would soon advance onto the central stage of history and determine the fate of the Chinese nation through their own struggles for truth, path, and identity. The most radical of them would turn to Marxism-Leninism, form the Chinese Communist Party (CCP), cut off connections to the Chinese tradition as much as they could, and commit to the complete remaking of the Chinese people. Most of the less radical but nonetheless politically committed would join the Nationalist Party (KMT). Originally conceived with inspiration from American-style democracy but also receiving aid and influence from the Soviet Union, the KMT sought to build up a new nation-state of China that retained much of its traditional heritage, –not as auniversal value but as its national distinction. The two parties' competition for political power in China would work itself out in epic scale in the middle decades of the century, ultimately resulting in the KMT's spectacular failure in 1949, and the CCP's takeover of the country, with Mao Zedong (1893–1976) as its supreme leader.

Zhang was a moderate product of this eventful and radicalized age. He received a mixed traditional and modern education, committed to nationalism and joined the KMT, pursued and received formal academic training in the US, and on his return to China became an influential scholar who closely followed—and sometimes became involved in—the politics of the Nationalist Party. As a modern intellectual, his view of and approach to his native place bore a strong resemblance to the literati of old. He took it as a place of home, recognized his roots therein, and was determined to return to it after his journey into the outside world.

However, responding to the changing times, he also sought to explore a path of electoral local politics by building on the tradition of literati localism. The KMT's political debacle cut short his experiment. In 1949, when the KMT lost the civil war and retreated to Taiwan, Zhang followed along and resettled his family on the island. There, during the following four decades of the Cold War and complete separation between Taiwan and the Chinese mainland, he and other sojourners from Anyang longed for and anticipated a return to their native place.

When Zhang died in 1988, the Cold War was nearing its end, and relations between the two regimes on either side of the Taiwan strait were thawing. The surviving sojourners finally returned to their native land in the late 1980s and early 1990s, only to find out that the native place that they knew and left behind had long since been destroyed under Communist rule. What remained was no longer recognizable. In a sense, both the natives staying in Anyang and the Anyang sojourners in Taiwan eventually became local-less, though for the latter, the death of the hometown took longer to be fully realized. To better understand the scope of their loss and the significance of the efforts made by people like Zhang, let us now delve deeper into history and see how, in the old days, the literati of Anyang lived their lives as locally rooted gentlemen of the world.

3.

The ruling class in China had been called the "*shi*" since before the establishment of the continental empire in the third century BCE. In Western literature, this term is often translated as the "literati." In its millennium-long history, the literati's social and cultural disposition went through profound transformations. One of the most significant of these occurred during the transition between the Tang (618 CE–907 CE) and the Song (960 CE–1276 CE) dynasty.

During this period, the establishment of a fully developed civil service examination system led to a major shift: success in the examinations became a standard requirement for access to and promotion within civil service, which was the most important criterion for elite status and the primary path to political power in China. The semi-hereditary aristocracy that had previously dominated civil service was soon replaced by a more fluid class of new men whose success depended not on heredity but on current officeholding, and eventually on the much less predictable examination outcomes. This transformation made the literati somewhat akin to the self-made gentry in England during the late medieval and early modern periods. Indeed, modern scholars have borrowed that term, referring to this new type of social elite in China as the "Chinese gentry."

As the newly modeled examination system penetrated deeply into local societies, it became both possible and increasingly necessary for almost all literati to begin the examination process in their local counties and prefectures. Consequently, the new ruling class—the gentry—became fundamentally oriented toward the local societies of their home places. For one, these local areas were where their civil service careers necessarily began, through participation in the lower-level examinations. Additionally, the unpredictability of examination success made it a strategic move for the gentry to focus on building social connections and influence within their home locales. This not only provided a strong local base in case their desired examination success did not materialize, but also ensured that they and their family members had a reliable foundation from which to continue attempting the examinations. Unlike the semi-aristocratic class of the previous period, who mostly resided in the capital region, the gentry steadily adopted a localist orientation. As one modern scholar put it, from the second half of the Song dynasty at the latest, the gentry had become political elites who "married locally, lived locally, and in many ways thought and acted locally."[2]

To support their locally based social life and career patterns, the gentry developed various strategies that modern scholars have described as "localist." These included compiling local gazetteers to celebrate the history and accomplishments of their regions, establishing marriage networks within the local society, and actively participating in public affairs within their communities. Over time, these localist strategies and activities transformed the localities—originally mere administrative entities of the state—into true home places for the gentry.

The most effective and enduring localist strategy, sometimes referred to as the localist strategy par excellence, was the construction of local lineages—organized kinship groups within local societies. Kinship organization had a long history in China and was deeply integrated with the Chinese tradition of ancestral worship and the Confucian concept of filial piety. Since all kin are the descendants of the same (paternal) ancestor, the rituals of ancestral worship and the ethics of filial piety could all be utilized in organizing kinsmen into cohesive social groups. During the age of feudalism, before the establishment of the unified empire, political power was hereditary and limited to aristocrats, making kinship identity—membership in the aristocratic clans—a crucial ticket to office. This hereditary privilege persisted to a substantial degree among the semi-aristocrats during the so-called Age of Division (fourth to seventh centuries) and continued into the Tang dynasty. Thus, marking kin group members and demarcating kin group boundaries, usually through compiling clan genealogies, became crucial for preserving the privileges of the aristocratic and semi-aristocratic clans. In other words, up until the Song dynasty, the practice of organizing kin groups was limited to the privileged few and followed an exclusivist orientation.

By the Song, with the rise of the gentry and their localist orientation, a new type of kin group organization emerged. With hereditary access to office no longer available, maintaining local influence and standing became crucial for the gentry. This necessity led them to unite their kinsmen within local societies, pooling resources and fostering mutual bonds. Consequently, gentry-led lineages began to form, aiming to include as many members of the kin group as possible who lived in the same area.

The development of this type of lineage took centuries of exploration and experimentation to establish viable organizational forms. To simplify a complex and lengthy history, one could say that by the time these lineages fully matured in the Ming (1368–1644) and Qing (1644–1911) dynasties, they typically featured three key elements (though at ground-level, not all practices were always present in all lineages):

a) Ritual unity through collective burials and/or a common ancestral hall;
b) Economic foundation through an incorporated lineage estate, which provided funds for lineage projects such as charity for the poor and education for the young; and
c) Kinship identity iteration through periodically renewed genealogies of the kin group.

This type of local lineage, through its ability to cultivate a shared identity among kinsmen living in the same area, had the power to intertwine the processes of local identity formation and kinship identity formation, making them mutually reinforcing. This is because lineage building had the potential of transforming the place of the gentry's initial career success into their ancestral home and place of dwelling. If the civil service examination system led their careers necessarily to begin in their native places, the lineage system could ensure that they would eventually return there at the end of their careers. Thus, the localist orientation of the gentry could gain ritual significance and moral depth, and become solemn.

We can see such solemnity in the ancestral instructions left by Han Qi, an Anyang native of the Sng dynasty who served as a prime minister and was a precursor of gentry localism. In a poem addressed to his descendants, Han urged all members of the Han clan to avoid moving away from their native place or being buried elsewhere. He emphasized that only in the native soil could one truly find a home:

> with ancestors stay, never forego 得从祖考游，
> find peace quietly, in the soul 魂魄自宁处.

4.

We have detailed information about two literati from Anyang during the late imperial period: Cui Xian (1478–1541) of the Ming dynasty, and Ma Piyao (1831–1895) of the Qing dynasty. Both men earned the highest degree of *jinshi* in the civil service examinations and held high-level offices in the state, establishing connections and exerting influence beyond their home locale. This makes them comparable to Zhang in terms of social status and scope of influence. However, China's position in the world changed significantly during the 500 years that span the lives of these three men. A brief examination of their life trajectories may help to place Zhang's life and efforts in a broader historical perspective.

Cui's time was the golden days of the Sinocentric world order. China had no rivalry in the world. Domestically, its social and political institutions were fully matured, and their limitations and problems had not been fully exposed. Political culture at the highest level was not as encouraging as some of the thriving historical periods, mostly due to the confrontations between the despotic power of the emperors and the moralistic approaches of the literati.³ Some literati, such as the great philosopher Wang Yangming (1472–1529), sought new ways to fulfill their noble duty of maintaining the social and moral order by working within local societies and engaging with the people, rather than staying in the court as direct assistants to the emperor, as orthodox teachings prescribed.

But that was far from a crisis of the civilization. From its own perspective, China was still the only true civilization in the world, and there was a sense of security and self-complacency in its views of other peoples living beyond its pale. Cui himself wrote condescendingly about the Hmong people on the southwest border of the Ming empire: they were "transformable" and could be civilized if the local officials (who were Chinese Confucian literati like himself) worked diligently and followed the right methods.⁴ This superior confidence was not without reason. Cui's essays, for example, were admired in places as far away as Korea, one of the most devoted members of the Sinocentric world order. During this era, classical Chinese was the universal language of this world, just as the Confucian teachings were its universal moral principles.

In terms of temperament, Cui Xian was more of a scholar than an administrator. Over his 36-year career as an official, beginning with his *jinshi* degree at age 27, he never served as the chief executive officer of a local jurisdiction. His posts were primarily related to literary and ritual functions: reader-in-waiting in the Royal Academy, chancellor of a National University, vice supervisor to the heir-apparent of the throne, and eventually vice minister of Rites. These roles involved advising and admonishing the emperor on various matters, which often required considerable moral courage. Cui did indeed risk his career and life by challenging the will of the throne on several occasions. Fortunately, he managed to survive the purges and persecutions that were common at the time. Despite this, the difficult conditions led him to adopt a strategy of distancing himself from the court. He began petitioning for retirement at the relatively young age of 39. Although the court was reluctant to let him go and occasionally recalled him, he ultimately spent 24 of his 36 post-*jinshi* years living in retreat in Anyang.

The conventional view that a literati, especially one with a *jinshi* degree, should serve as the emperor's assistant troubled Cui Xian. Even when away from the court, he frequently pondered the meaning of life for a learned gentleman in retreat. In response to an imagined challenge to his decision to leave the court, Cui argued that those who risk their lives to admonish the emperor might merely be seeking fame rather than embodying true loyalty. A gentleman, according to Cui, does not need to be a conformist to seek harmony, nor does he need to rely on extremist arguments for distinction. What is essential is to understand what is right in the world and promote it. For Cui, the essence of a learned gentleman's life in retreat lies in the concept of moral autonomy. Despite forces beyond one's control, moral autonomy allows a gentleman to distance himself from the Son-of-Heaven's court while remaining steadfast in his pursuit of moral truth.

Cui Xian's life in Anyang was comfortable, leisurely, and dignified. As a retired court official, he earned respect from both local officials and literati. The prefect of Zhangde Prefecture, which included Anyang as the primary county, even asked Cui to name his newborn child. Local government school instructors regularly led their students to his home to pay their respects. Scholars traveled long distances to study with him. In return for these honors, Cui single-handedly compiled the Zhangde Prefectural gazetteer at the prefect's invitation and frequently wrote essays commemorating local events, such as the opening of new community schools.

Privately, Cui engaged in lineage building, working on a genealogy and constructing an ancestral shrine for his clan. His family owned a modest farm of about 30 acres outside the county seat, where he spent most of his time gardening and studying. He even wrote an essay specifically about his life there, entitled "On Dwelling":

> I resigned again and returned home. South of the [irrigation] canal, I have a small farm where we grow grains and vegetables, relying on them for sustenance and nourishment. I call on fellow countrymen and kinsmen to join me in cultivating loyalty and trustworthiness, illuminating the Dao of benevolence and righteousness, and practicing good manners in social interactions. I promote the writings of Master Zhu [Xi] and carefully study works by other Sung dynasty scholars. I explore the causes of order and chaos in past eras and also learn about medicine, agronomy, divination, and horticulture. In my spare time, I gather friends and relatives for drinking parties. When in good spirits, we contemplate the subtle meanings of things or compose essays and poetry.

All of Cui Xian's activities—learning, lineage building, ritual practicing, engaging in moral cultivation, teaching, and participating in community leadership—were aligned with the expectations of a gentleman of the world. They can all be regarded as the first steps in ordering the world, for if one local place can be transformed through these endeavors, other places might follow, eventually leading to an orderly "all-under-heaven." In this sense, Cui's local life in Anyang carried universalistic connotations. Far from being merely provincial, his life had a cosmopolitan quality. Although he experienced some initial unease, he eventually found contentment in this way of life. This may explain why Cui was so devoted to it. Less than a year into his final service post in Nanjing, he petitioned for retirement due to signs of illness and set out for home as soon as his petition was approved. He died shortly after arriving home. According to local custom, it was considered a good death, as he passed away in his native place.

Ma Piyao's temperament and career trajectory were almost the exact opposite of Cui Xian's. A capable and energetic administrator, Ma consistently held executive roles throughout his career. Over his 30-year post-*jinshi* career, Ma remained in office nearly all the time, with only two leaves for mourning his father and stepmother. Far from being disillusioned by his administrative duties, Ma saw his career marked by optimism and success. He died while serving as the governor of Guangdong Province. Despite their differing career paths, Cui and Ma shared a similar view of their home place. For both, life in their native locale, with its ancestral rituals and kinship organization, was seen as profoundly meaningful and the final destination. Although Ma's official duties kept him away from home for most of his career, his intention to return to his native place was clear from an early age. A poem he wrote at age 17, while still a student in Anyang, expressed his ambition: "To assist the king, sweeping the world and saving lives; then return home, to the mountains, wine, poetry, and an unrestrained life." While this youthful vision of a carefree life has Daoist undertones, the mature Ma never shirked his responsibilities to his kinsmen or his native place.

As the first *jinshi* and official of the Ma clan, he took care of not only his own children but also other promising kids of the clan. He brought Jidong, the son of a cousin, to his service place for better education. In 1885, he donated 2,000 taels as the initial fund for the construction of a joint ancestral shrine of the Ma clan, which was made up of two branches by then. It was Jidong, together with Piyao's son Jishen, who carried the fund home from Taiyuan where Piyao was posted. In addition to the shrine, Ma contributed 9,000 taels to fund a lineage estate for his own branch of the clan. This estate was intended to provide charitable relief to kinsmen in need, with Jidong appointed as the managing head, and Jishen as his deputy. Ma also invested most of his income into building a family complex in his home village. In 1892, while staying home for the mourning of his stepmother, Ma purchased a small estate near his childhood home and began planning long-term improvements, likely in preparation for his retirement. Simultaneously, he began drafting instructions for his sons on how to preserve and grow the family's fortunes through hard work and vigilance.

As an influential and capable official, Ma was capable of intervening in the bureaucracy to advocate for and assist his home community. For their part, the local gentry in Anyang were ready to call on Ma's service whenever they needed him. One notable example was his involvement in resolving a long-standing issue with the official requisition of transportation services in Anyang. The county, situated on a key transportation artery, was frequently burdened with requisitions that caused considerable hardship for the local community. The management of these requisitions by local clerks was notorious for corruption and exploitation. The Anyang gentry, seeking to address this issue, proposed creating an independent Bureau of Carts and Horses to handle the requisitions more fairly. However, this proposal clashed with the interests of the clerks and faced resistance from the local magistrate, leading to an almost riotous situation in 1885. In this critical moment, the Anyang gentry turned to Ma Piyao for assistance. Ma's intervention, involving communication with higher-level authorities, ultimately led to a resolution of the conflict and alleviated the burden on the local community. Ma's role in addressing another local issue further illustrates his dedication. When local officials in Zhangde Prefecture imposed pressure on landlords for subscriptions to a government-sponsored grain storage project, the local gentry complained about the undue pressure and tight deadlines. Ma Piyao responded by directly writing to the prefect, urging him to instruct the magistrate of Anyang County to grant an extension on the subscription deadline.

If we just look at the way they view and engage the home place, there is hardly any indication of the change in time between Cui's mid-Ming and Ma's late-Qing. Yet Ma did live in a very different time. By the time he earned his *jinshi* degree in 1862, the Qing dynasty had been defeated twice by Britain in the Opium Wars and forced to recognize the Western powers as equals. Strictly speaking, that was the official end of the Sinocentric world order, though in people's minds some time was still needed to make sense of the change. By the time Ma died in 1895, the first Sino-Japanese war was about to end with the Qing's devastating defeat. This was a defeat much more shocking than all the wars the Qing had lost during the previous half century, for the harsh concessions Japan imposed but more for the psychological effect, that a "little brother" on the margin of the Sinocentric world was able to rout the Qing military so thoroughly and humiliate the Central Country so relentlessly. Real reforms that led to the dismantling of the old regime started soon after that. So, Ma's time can be called the beginning of the end of the traditional Chinese civilization.

Most of the last ten years of his career were spent serving as the governor of the southwestern province of Guangxi. There, he also faced issues related to the Hmong people. Unlike Cui, who viewed them as barbarians to be civilized, Ma referred to them simply as "people," comparable to the Chinese in the heartland. This shift in perspective reflects the impact of several centuries of Qing assimilation policies. However, a more prominent cultural "other" emerged during Ma's time: the French in Vietnam. In the 1880s, the French had pulled Vietnam out of the Sinocentric system and established it as a colony. The French government then invited the Qing jointly to survey the border region and accurately demarcate the border between China and Vietnam. As Guangxi bordered Vietnam, Ma was assigned the task of overseeing this international cooperation project. At the age of 60, Ma personally undertook a tour of several hundred miles along the border. Such serious attention was characteristic of Qing officials dealing with foreign affairs in the late nineteenth century, who, having learned through painful experience about the power of Western nations, exercised extreme caution and vigilance.

The sense of superiority once held by the Central Country had dissipated. This shift was due not only to the equality protocols imposed by Western countries but also to the personal experience of Qing officials. Ma expressed the difficulties of cooperating with the French in a letter to a senior colleague, noting that the lack of mutual trust often stemmed from both sides' nervousness and fear of being looked down upon. In another letter, Ma referenced the recent Franco-Prussian War to encourage one of his subordinates to boost the morale of the troops. He argued that morale, more than weaponry or the size of the country, is crucial for victory, citing Prussia's triumph over the larger France as an example. He used the term *ren he*, meaning "harmony of the people," a concept in Chinese parlance that denotes the result of benevolent rule by a sage ruler. This indicates that the new "other" for the Central Country, the modern West, was seen as capable of achieving high moral standards comparable to those of the legendary sage kings of China.

Although Ma never expressed admiration for the West's powers straightforwardly, his writings provide unequivocal signs that the latter evoked awe in him. The nervousness his colleagues felt in the day-to-day interactions with the French probably stemmed from the same mindset. It is hard to imagine the French felt as nervous as the Chinese and shared the latter's fear of being looked down upon. Most likely it was Ma who created this facade of parity, just to preserve some dignity of a Sinocentric mindset.

The times were indeed changing. In 1872, James Legge, a British missionary to China and translator of Chinese classics, captured the essence of this transformation in his writings:

> During the past forty years her [i.e., China's] position with regard to the more advanced nations of the world has entirely changed. She has entered into treaties with them upon equal terms; but I do not think her ministers and people have yet looked the truth fairly in the face, so as to realize the fact that China is only one of many independent nations in the world, and that the "beneath the sky" [the same *tianxia*] over which her emperor has ruled, is not all beneath the sky, but only a certain portion of it which is defined on the earth's surface and can be pointed out upon the map. But if they will not admit this, and strictly keep good faith according to the treaties which they have accepted, the result will be for the calamities greater than any that have yet befallen the empire. [5]

More changes were on the horizon. How to navigate these changes and what to retain from the past became a pressing challenge for the younger generations in Anyang and throughout China.

1
The new world

When Zhang Jinjian was born in 1902, much of the imagined and ritualized "all-under-heaven" world of China had changed. Interactions with Western powers over the previous eight decades had substantially exposed the country to a new, geographically verifiable world centered in the modern West. China was forcefully dragged into a situation where it became a marginal part, along with other Asian and African countries. Meanwhile, various aspects of Western culture seeped in. For example, the Copernican universe of Western science collided with and eventually invalidated Chinese cosmological ideas of "yin" and "yang" and "heaven" and "earth." The consequences of such a "world change" were profound and tectonic when viewed with historical hindsight.

The same year Zhang was born, Kang Youwei (1858–1927), a middle-aged scholar from Guangdong Province, finished his *One World Philosophy*. Wrapped in Confucian language, it announced that the so-called three bonds—the bonds between father and son, husband and wife, and emperor and subjects, which had been assumed by Confucian orthodoxy to be the eternal pattern of human relationships mandated by Heaven, and served as the foundation of the social and political order—were nothing more than products of circumstantial social forces. It claimed that filial piety—the virtue of all virtues in Confucian society—was rather a social institution suited to a particular time. The tremendous sense of liberation (and confusion) that this announcement delivered would resonate for decades among the educated youth, including Mao Zedong, the would-be founder of the People's Republic of China (PRC). For this reason, Kang is sometimes credited with initiating China's modern ideology.

Also, in 1902, Kang's most famous student, Liang Qichao (1873–1929), began writing newspaper articles in Japan that were eventually collected as *The New People*. In it, Liang called on the Chinese to reimagine themselves, not as subjects of the emperor, nor as kin of a family or clan, nor even as humans of the "all-under-heaven," but as citizens of the nation-state of China. The reason, Liang explained, was that, due to specific circumstances in the past, the Chinese did not recognize the existence of parallel civilizations, equivalent peoples, or peer states beyond their own horizon. Yet the world has always been a place of competition for survival among peoples, a competition in which the loser risks extinction. In the new century, this struggle had become fiercer, and the only viable unit in this competition is a state formed by a distinctive national people—that is, the nation-state. Thus, to avoid being eliminated as a loser, China must become a nation-state, and the Chinese must cultivate civic virtues and participate in public affairs as citizens. Liang's powerful writings would become a crucial source of inspiration in the rise of Chinese nationalism. He had to go into exile in Japan because the radical reforms he and Kang helped the young emperor launch in 1898 offended the empress dowager, who held real power in the dynasty.

Neither Kang nor Liang was against monarchy in general or the Manchu Qing dynasty specifically. Rather, they envisioned a constitutional monarchy with the Manchu court as the head of the newly conceptualized Chinese nation-state. However, the ground had shifted. More and more people were realizing that the order of things was no longer that people should prove their loyalty to the dynasty, but rather that the dynasty must prove itself useful for the survival of the national people. As the Qing dynasty continued to lose wars to Western (and Japanese) powers and make more concessions, pressures mounted for the Qing dynasty to reform itself. The biggest disaster came in 1900, when peasants in northern China, driven by xenophobia caused by the spread of Christianity, rose in hundreds of small bands to kill foreigners and Chinese Christians. The empress dowager, seeing an opportunity to utilize the peasant force and expel foreign powers from China, supported the rebels and declared war on all foreign powers. The result was a total humiliation, culminating in the occupation of Beijing by the allied forces of eight powers. After that, it became clear that the old ways would not work; substantial changes, not only at the technical level as the dynasty had allowed during the previous decades, but also in political institutions and orthodox learning, were necessary. The series of reforms that ensued during the last decade of the Qing would drastically change the imperial polity and—since they were pushed through in such a hasty manner—also contribute to the dynasty's own collapse.

Particularly relevant to Zhang's life were the reforms in education and civil service recruitment. In 1902, the court decreed reforms to the civil service examination system, starting with curriculum changes and planning to phase it out completely in ten years.

Two years later, a decree on the new school system was issued, and Western-style schools began to be founded across the country. Then, in 1905, the Japanese victory in the Russo-Japanese War—a bloody conflict between a westernized Asian country and an established European power fought in the Qing dynasty's ancestral homeland of Manchuria—shocked the dynasty once again and prompted it to rush forward with the reforms, abolishing the civil service examinations immediately. Thus, the cornerstone of the imperial system, which had regulated upward mobility, maintained social order, and buttressed orthodox learning and morality for about a thousand years, was suddenly gone before most of the educated class was ready. For the hundreds of thousands of men invested in this career path, it must have felt the same as what one of them wrote in his diary, that he received the news "with a heart like ashes."[6]

Zhang was too young to bear the brunt of these changes directly. However, his life would be shaped by the fallout from such deep and hasty transformations. First, at the individual level, there arose a much more complicated scenario regarding life and career trajectories. With the dismantling of the examination system, orthodox learning and traditional education were no longer tied to civil service (i.e., the gold standard of upward mobility). Now, educated individuals had to figure out new ways of defining a meaningful life and pursuing a worthy career. Diplomas from the new-style schools could be aligned with the degrees from the old examination system, but the establishment of new schools progressed at a much slower pace than the issuance of decrees from the court. By the time the Qing dynasty collapsed in 1911, Anyang County had only one new-style elementary school and one middle school within the county seat, both established by the local authorities. Beyond the county seat, only one of the county's nine rural districts had a new-style elementary school. The vast majority of school-aged children still received their education through traditional homeschooling, based on traditional curricula. This meant they were educated in subjects with which most people felt emotionally comfortable, but which were not necessarily applicable to the future.

Zhang started homeschooling at age ten. The homeschools he attended included one in his home village, about ten miles west of the county seat, and another in the county seat, taught by a relative who held a *jinshi* degree from the civil service examination system. Over the course of seven years, he was trained to read and memorize the key Confucian classics, practice couplet parallelism and poetry, and compose essays—all standard components of the examination-oriented curriculum of the past. These experiences might have anchored his personal life in the old ways. However, for a career in the new world, he would need to learn new things at the new schools. The same year his homeschooling began, the Qing dynasty collapsed and was replaced by a republic. Since the emperor in traditional China was not only the head of a dynastic state but also regarded as the linchpin between Heaven, Earth, and the human world, the abolition of the monarchy also dissolved much of the cosmological symbolism. Consequently, the Chinese universe of meaning inevitably felt the disruptive impact. Many people who were deeply entrenched in traditional learning found themselves unable to adjust to the new world, with some even choosing not to continue living. While Zhang's traditional education might still bring him some cultural prestige in certain circles, in the long run, it could lead to more dissonance and incongruity.

The political environment of the country changed dramatically after the Qing dynasty's collapse. The dynasty was abandoned partly because it failed to defend the newly conceptualized Chinese nation. However, the young republic did not establish a strong foundation for the nation either. If anything, the situation worsened, as the old power center of the court was gone and no viable new political center had been established in its place, leading the country to deteriorate into rampant warlordism. With no alien dynasty to blame, the built-up pressure of nationalist sentiment among Chinese intellectuals vented its steam on their own cultural tradition. The devastating force that had been latent since Kang Youwei's announcement was now fully released, giving rise to totalistic anti-traditionalism in the early years of the republic. Alongside the condemnation of Chinese tradition, various new ideas and ideologies—including liberalism, socialism, anarchism, communism, and feminism—were introduced from the West to fill the vacuum it left behind. As a result, China's intellectual culture became radicalized. People referred to these radical cultural changes during the decade or so beginning in the mid-1910s as the "New Culture Movement."

Some of the key carriers of the new culture, such as the *New Youth* magazine published in Beijing by the leading intellectuals of the day, were brought to Anyang and circulated among the teachers and students at the middle school. The county got its first modern newspaper in the last year of the Qing dynasty, and two more in the first several years of the republic. Even common folks in Anyang, who were not familiar with literary culture, would have seen enough signs to know that times had changed. For example, missionaries from Canada's Presbyterian Church had been working in Anyang and other North Henan counties since the last decade of the nineteenth century. By the time the Republic of China was founded in 1912, they had established one hospital and two middle schools, one of which was specifically for girls. The missionaries brought their wives and daughters with them, and men and women worked together. A newspaper published in Shanghai during the last years of the Qing dynasty recorded how local Chinese perceived the way missionaries from the West treated their womenfolk. People in Anyang must have witnessed this with the same amazement:

> We often observe Western couples; whenever they are together, they always hold each other's hands. When they take a seat, they sit side by side, and when they dine together, they engage in conversation—whether about grand ideas, books, current political affairs, or other news. They respect each other as honored guests and cooperate like geese that fly and sing together in order, all the way until the end of their lives. Isn't this what is referred to in Confucian classics as "ordering the family"?[7]

Even among Chinese women in Anyang, some—though not many—were becoming public and independent. Ma Piyao's daughter Qingxia (1877–1922) was one of them. She married the heir to one of the biggest landholdings in the province and became the sole inheritor of great wealth when her husband died young and childless. Bored and tired of the petty harassment from her begrudging in-laws, she joined her older brother,

Piyao's second son and a court official, on his official duty as a diplomat to Japan. There, she was introduced to a circle of revolutionaries among the Chinese diaspora who sought to overthrow the Qing dynasty and turn their country into a republic. It was an eye-opening experience. As if suddenly enlightened on how to spend the fortune under her name, Qingxia became one of the most generous donors to the revolutionary movement, sponsoring their organizations, publications, and sometimes their rebellious activities. She became a friend of Sun Yat-sen, the founder of the Republic of China, and donated her entire fortune to his cause. Toward the end of her life in the early 1920s, having earned herself the fame of a Republican heroine and completely alienated from her husband's family, Qingxia returned to her native place of Anyang and lived in her ancestral home for a few years before her death.

New elements in the economy were rapidly emerging at the turn of the new century in Anyang and other places. After the treaty of 1895, signed at the end of the first Sino-Japanese War, foreigners were allowed to open factories in China. Soon, Chinese-owned modern factories also began to emerge. The first one in Anyang was a cotton textile mill, cofounded in 1903 by Ma Piyao's oldest son, Ma Jishen (1857–1912). In the same year, Jishen also invested in a new coal mine in Anyang, utilizing modern mining technologies and imported foreign machinery. The new mining company was located in Liuhegou village, 20 miles northwest of the county seat, and it soon became one of the largest coal mines in the whole country. Then, in 1906, the railway linking Beijing and the central China metropolis of Wuhan was opened. This railway came to be the most important transportation artery in the country. It established a major station in Anyang and significantly changed the economic dynamics of the region. For example, cotton growers in the county could now ship their products directly to the Beijing-Tianjin area where foreign textile factories were eager for raw materials, rather than being limited to the local market.

Given the changing times, education in the new-style schools seemed inevitable. However, admission to the reputable public middle school in the county seat was highly competitive. Therefore, at age 17, Zhang enrolled at a private preparatory middle school in the provincial capital Kaifeng. There, he had his first taste of modern education: new subjects such as English and mathematics, and military training—due to the surging nationalism in the early Republican era that advocated a strong militarist culture—and the excitement of participating in public protests, which were becoming more frequent in the young Republic of China.

One year later, in 1920, Zhang made it back to Anyang, successfully passed the entrance exam, and was admitted by the county's middle school. Zhang would study for five years (one year in the foundation program, four years in the regular program) in this school. In his memoir, written at age 70, he called this period the "golden age" of his life. His scores in regular courses remained at the top of his class in all semesters; his conduct and sports performance were all assessed as superb. What's more impressive were his extracurricular activities. He was the undisputed leader of student government. Together with other students, the student government successfully expelled a sexually misbehaving faculty member at the school. He was also elected chair of the united student government of schools in the whole north Henan region centered around Anyang, as well as president of the local activist group called the "Unbound Foot Society," which advocated the termination of female foot-binding. With the continued rise of nationalism across the country in the 1920s, he became the main organizer of student protests, against warlord politics as well as Japanese aggression. In 1925, the May Thirtieth Incident occurred in Shanghai, whereby a confrontation between the Chinese labor movement and foreign factory owners led to the killing of dozens of striking workers. It triggered an intense wave of anti-imperialist protests across the country, and many cities organized local anti-imperialist unions. The protest in Anyang was led by none other than Zhang, a senior at the local middle school.

The teachers and headmaster of the school appreciated Zhang so much that they entrusted him with a task they deemed significant and, properly speaking, their own: the founding of a charity school to provide free education for local children who were deprived of access to modern education due to the insufficient number of new-style elementary schools. With the help of his teachers, Zhang was able to raise substantial funds from the nearby military garrison, purchase some land, and construct a new building for the school. Instructors were recruited from among his fellow students. Before Zhang's graduation, the charity school had successfully trained more than 100 students in three years.

Many of Zhang's teachers in middle school were among the first generation of intellectuals in China to receive a modern education, and they were the first to face the challenge of figuring out new paths forward for both life and career in the aftermath of the abolition of the examination system. Becoming a schoolteacher, one of the many modern professions, was a common choice due to the high demand for schools and modern education. Yet the political situation at the time was so provocative that it must have been difficult for these modern counterparts of the traditional literati to resist the perceived calls for political engagement. This is why so many political figures in the Republican era had stints as schoolteachers. Mao himself, nine years older than Zhang, attended the No. 1 Normal College in Hunan Province and served as the headmaster of an elementary school before his career took a sharp turn toward Communism. This general pattern is clearly exemplified by the teachers in Zhang's middle school. The military training instructor, Xu Xiangqian (1901–1990), was from Shanxi Province and would later become a field marshal in Communist China; the teacher of natural history, Zhao Zhichen, came from a nearby county and later served as the last minister of northern Henan during the Republican era, dying as a martyr when the Communists took over Anyang in 1949; and the physics teacher, Zhang Tianji, a native of Anyang, became the headmaster of the school after Zhang's graduation and was later elected chair of the Anyang County Council.

The high turnover of teachers in Zhang's middle school is not surprising, given their political aspirations. When Zhang graduated in June 1925, the school's headmaster, Chang Shouqi, an Anyang native, had already been appointed magistrate of Huojia County, located 90 miles to the southwest. In July, Zhang was invited to Huojia and began working as the magistrate's communication assistant. In October, the school's provost, Gong Peicheng, from

Jiangsu Province, was hired as an adviser to the commander of a military division stationed in Xinxiang County (which neighbors Huojia). Gong invited Zhang to join him, and there, Zhang got his second job as a staff member at the military division's headquarters, where he was responsible for propaganda work and mobilizing civilian support for the military. By 1925, the Nationalist Revolution was gathering momentum. Shortly before that, Sun Yat-sen—the founder of the Republic of China who had lost power after its founding—had decided to cooperate with the Soviet Union, to reform his Nationalist Party along Bolshevik lines, and to launch a military expedition to reunify the politically fragmented country. Gong, being a Nationalist Party member, was likely the reason this military leader based on his advice had become so politicized. However, soon the military division was redeployed elsewhere, and Gong himself undertook a new political mission to convert a military leader in Manchuria to the cause of the Nationalist Revolution. At this juncture, Wen Liangru, the school's Chinese teacher hailing from Shaanxi Province, was appointed magistrate of Anyang County and offered Zhang a position in the county government.

By January 1926, Zhang was back in Anyang, still holding the title of the magistrate's communication assistant. Since that position controlled the communication channel to the magistrate, it carried disproportionate power and was sometimes dubbed the "magistrate's deputy." This role, combined with Zhang's fame and experience as a student leader in previous years, as well as his skills in handling complicated situations, made him a significant figure in local society. For example, he was able to bring together his influential relatives from the countryside and leverage his special relationship with the magistrate to coordinate the militias from all ten districts for a successful anti-banditry campaign in the county. On another occasion, a hostile warlord laid siege to the county seat and demanded that the government open the walled city, threatening bombardment if his demands were not met. The magistrate happened to be away at the time. Zhang convened all the leading gentry (i.e., district heads) residing in town and devised a solution to the crisis. They allowed a district head to deliver the key to the gatekeeper, who then opened the city gate to avoid bloodshed while saving face for the magistrate.

Zhang himself admitted that while working in the Anyang County government, he was treated like a local grandee despite his young age. Living in the county, he was able to provide substantial benefits to his kinsmen and relatives in the countryside. He served on the board of trustees of the county's first private middle school. His official salary as a communication assistant was 30 silver dollars, but his unofficial income from "conventional" offerings from local society could be six or seven times that amount.

However, Zhang was not satisfied with such a comfortable life. He decided to apply to Beijing University, the top university in the country, and was admitted. Thus, in September 1926, just 9 months after returning to Anyang and 15 months after graduating from middle school, he left again. Regarding his motivation for this decision, his memoir simply states, "one cannot be complacent with the present condition and disregard the future." Judging from the style of his diary and his memoir, Zhang appeared to be a man of practical energy rather than deep self-reflection. However, perhaps little reflection was needed in this case. A capable young man would naturally have greater expectations than a comfortable life close to home. In any case, the decision was consequential. Unlike his previous brief journeys within Henan Province, this move would launch his career into a much larger world and lead his life faraway from home.

Zhang would return to Anyang many times throughout his career and planned to retire there toward the end of his life. This pattern is not unlike that of the literati, such as Cui and Ma, in the old days. However, the trajectory of his life and career would be very different after he entered the larger world. His diplomas, whether from the middle school in Anyang or future ones from more advanced institutions, were insufficient to grant him elite status in the way that examination degrees conferred upon the literati of the past.

The late Qing reformers had allowed modern school diplomas to be matched to examination degrees, but the Qing dynasty had collapsed fifteen years before. Even if the Qing had survived, this specific policy would have had no chance of creating the same effects as the civil service examinations, because the civil service examination system produced a unitary ruling class defined by the same knowledge, social values, and service in a universal state. Mere participation in the examination system was enough to initiate one into that country-wide ruling class, earning respect in local society and dignified treatment from officials, who were molded by the same matrix and through the same procedures. What the late Qing reforms abolished was not just the monopoly of truth held by orthodox learning, but also the alignment between learning and service. Now, no form of learning necessarily led to participation in the state, and no social group was by default considered the ruling class.

Zhang's successful life and career in Anyang and the nearby counties since his graduation no doubt benefited from his middle school education. But that probably had less to do with his diploma than with his personal capability and his special connections with his teachers. Indeed, he never even mentioned a "diploma" in his memoir. In Anyang during the early 1920s when he had his "golden age," social and political power was no longer simply shared between the court-appointed magistrate and the examination-tested literati-gentry. The bureaucrats, the warlords, the old-style gentry, the new style intellectuals, and even the bandits were all competing for dominance in an unsettled world. In fact, when the Communists eventually took over Anyang in 1949, the military leaders of the defense forces were mostly former bandits who were co-opted by the KMT government.

When Zhang left Anyang for the larger world, he was not following a known track of civil service like Cui and Ma did in their days. Instead, he plunged into uncertainty, for he had no clear idea what an education from (let alone a diploma from) Beijing University could bring him or where it could lead him. For its part, Beijing University would have no way to guarantee its graduates an elite status despite its high reputation, for it was just one of many universities in the country, none of which, as educational instead of ritual institutions, had the authority to distribute official title and social status as the examination system did in the old days. Uncertainty was the price for the termination of the examination system that each educated person had to pay at the individual level.

Society as a whole paid a different price for this change: the fragmentation of the educated class. In the old days, the literati-gentry, as the ruling class, faced various problems such as factionalism and corruption, but they were able to maintain a basic social and intellectual cohesion, however precarious it may have been. There was one set of moral standards centered on the virtues of filiality and loyalty, one meaningful career goal as educated gentlemen—crystallized in assisting the monarch in ordering the world—and one accepted understanding of the cosmos and humanity found in the Confucian classics. Now that the monarchy, the civil service examination, and the sacred status of orthodox learning were all gone, people no longer had to learn or believe in the same things or pursue the same goals. Educated individuals in society no longer constituted a single class.

Zhang's generation of educated youth in Anyang, for example, demonstrated a diversity of career paths and intellectual trajectories that could have astounded their literati predecessors. Among those who left traces in history were Guo Shengyong (1904–1929), Zhang's best friend and sworn brother from middle school, who received only traditional homeschooling; Ma Zai (1905–1992), another schoolmate whose education up to that point combined homeschooling and new-style elementary school; and Xie Guozhen (1901–1982), who skipped both elementary and middle school, instead receiving relatively complete classical training through private tutoring. At age 25, he was directly admitted to the graduate program at the prestigious National Learning Institute of Tsinghua University, where his adviser was none other than the prominent Liang Qichao.

Zhang eventually became a university professor dabbling in party politics. In his memoir he stated that his occupation is "*shi*," whose pursuit in life is the "*dao*" (lit. the Way). Here the "*shi*" is the same appellation the literati had called themselves, whose pursuit of the "*dao*" instead of material gains set them apart as the noble people who deserved to lead the rest of society and be respected by them. But following this self-identification Zhang immediately provided his own definition of "*dao*," which he took as simply "knowledge." That assertion separated him from the literati, for whom the "*dao*" was first and foremost a moral aspiration, and squarely put him back among modern professionals devoted to objective knowledge production and transmission. But at least a professorial occupation bears some resemblance to that of the traditional literati, for Confucius himself was a teacher with political aspirations and visions. Upon graduation, Guo and Ma both decided to pursue a military career, something the literati had looked down upon for centuries. They both went to Guangdong and enrolled in the Huangpu Military Academy Sun Yat-sen founded with the grand plan of militarily reunifying the country, and both indeed lived their dreams of becoming military officers. Xie ended up a reputed antiquarian and historian, and after the Communist takeover spent the majority of his life as research fellow at the National Academy of Social Sciences.

In addition to the diversified career paths, there emerged an unprecedented phenomenon of ideological conflict: unlike before, when educated individuals shared a common vision of an ideal society and largely the same approach to achieving it, people could now be educated at various institutions, committed to conflicting visions of the future, and approach their goals with drastically different and sometimes incompatible means. Influenced by his teachers Chang, Gong, and Wen, Zhang became a believer in Sun Yat-sen's Three Principles of the People and joined the Nationalist Party. In contrast, Ma and Guo were more influenced by the military instructor Xu Xiangqian and joined the Communist Party. Although the Soviet Union brokered a brief United Front between the two parties, the alliance ultimately broke down, leading them to become fierce adversaries. Guo was captured in battle while leading the Communist force against the Nationalist troops, and soon executed. Zhang lamented that his best friend had been misled by Communism. Xie, due to his mild and noncompetitive temperament, was ideologically noncommitted and did not join any political party. However, in the turbulent age of an agitated country, armchair scholars like Xie were destined to be marginalized. It is difficult to argue that in modern times, they carried the legacy of the literati elite of old.

Thus, the political culture nurtured for centuries by the literati class was gone. Their modern counterparts—the intellectuals—were fragmented in outlook and uncertain in social status. When Zhang and his cohorts moved beyond their hometown and entered the world, they could not help but become "roaming intellectuals" in the young Chinese republic, just like their teachers. They hopped from one place to another in the vast country, frequently changing employment along with their roles and viewpoints. In a time of political and intellectual turmoil, they had passion and ambition, albeit without any set goals or paths in life. Each of them would have to explore their own way forward. Much of China's fate would depend on the collective efforts of these two generations born shortly before or after the turn of the twentieth century.

Their private lifestyles were also diverse, even among those who shared comparable interests in politics. Those committed to Communism, for example, spent decades suppressing particularistic sentiments, such as those toward family and their native place. Zhang's involvement in student protests aligned him with the radical youth politically. However, he appeared to be a relatively conservative product of a radicalized age. He was comfortable with the idea and practice of filial piety, was close to both his parents, remained deeply attached to his family throughout his life, and genuinely enjoyed life in his hometown, where he was close to his kin. As the firstborn among his siblings, he received special love and care, which he reciprocated with his own thoughtfulness and sense of duty.

As a child, Zhang was particularly close to his grandmother, who raised and educated him while his mother was occupied with caring for his younger siblings. Grandma and grandson slept in the same bed, and she always placed some food beside his pillow so that the moment he woke up in the morning, he could eat. It was to make his grandmother happy that Zhang returned home after one semester at Beijing University to get married, as she wanted to see a great-grandchild.

The bride, Wang Songzu, from a nearby village, was proposed to him by a matchmaker, and Zhang had his first look at her on their wedding night. Before that, he was able to thoroughly enjoy the wedding ceremony. According to local custom, it included the procedure of the groom's family sending a receiving team to the bride's house, led by the horse-riding groom and carrying a sedan chair specifically decorated for bringing the bride back. After performing a set of rituals at the bride's house, the team then proceeded back to the groom's house, heralding the whole process with a musical band, continuous firecrackers, and ritual firearms intermittently shooting into the sky. The ceremony at the groom's house included the presentation of ritual objects (such as a mirror, water bottle, scale, and silk, each symbolizing a specific wifely virtue) to the bride by the women of the groom's family. The new couple bowed to the tablets of Heaven and Earth, and the bride bowed to her parents-in-law. Throughout the ceremony, the bride's head was covered with a red piece of cloth, which was to be unveiled by the groom in the bedchamber only before they consummated the marriage. Zhang remembered all the details of his wedding and was able to write them down in his memoir decades later. Clearly, the traditional way of getting married brought him joy instead of resentment.

The marriage proved to be a success. Zhang and his wife remained harmonious even after his supposedly "westernizing" experiences of studying in the US. Years later, his teacher Gong Peicheng was able to visit his home and was amazed to find that a US-trained professor was living in a happy marriage with his wife from a village in their native place. The success of the marriage undoubtedly helped further embed Zhang into the network of social relations in his hometown. In 1928, when he graduated from the Central Party Academy of the Nationalist Party and volunteered to work in the frontier region of Xinjiang, his father-in-law and paternal uncle traveled a long way to Nanjing, where the academy was located, to persuade him not to go, fearing that it would take him too far away from home. Given that there was no direct train line from Anyang to Nanjing, it took several days on the road in those times.

It is fair to say that Zhang was deeply rooted in his family and clan. From the very beginning, he felt comfortable and safe in his native place. His decision to move on and seek a career in the larger world does not suggest that he was alienated from his home. After all, locally oriented literati in the old days, such as Cui and Ma, also sought to pursue careers beyond their hometowns. As long as they maintained connections with their home place and eventually returned to it, they were always considered men of that place. As we shall see below, Zhang would maintain his connection to his native place in almost exactly the same way Cui and Ma did, planning for his retirement back home before he was forced to leave the Chinese mainland in 1949.

Even the quintessential localist strategy of the literati—that is, the lineage-building efforts that helped merge one's kinship identity with local identity, allowing them to enhance each other—can be seen in Zhang's case. Lineage building was a demanding enterprise that not all clans could afford. It required not only economic resources but also strong clan leadership, as it involved ritual activities, moral teachings, and organizational work. That is why, during the Ming and Qing dynasties, the emergence of a successful literati in a clan—typically a *jinshi* degree holder—often marked a leap forward in the clan's lineage-building project. Cui and Ma both played crucial roles in building their own lineages. Zhang's father was a capable farmer and part-time merchant, while his grandfather earned the lowest degree in the examination system during the Qing. Regarding social status, the clan was far from prosperous. The organization of their kinsmen was not highly developed, although some efforts had been made. Zhang's father maintained a pedigree chart of the clan, which could eventually develop into a full genealogy. Zhang praised his father for valuing this pedigree chart more than the deeds to their landholdings, a common commendation for lineage builders in the late imperial period. In his mature years, Zhang was devoted to establishing the Zhang family farm and sent any savings home for his father to purchase more land. Given the opportunity, Zhang would likely have engaged in a lineage-building project (modified by modern social conditions, as it almost certainly would be) for his clan, just as Cui and Ma did for theirs.

Yet the changing times were real, and they would significantly affect the evolution of his career. While his relationship to his native soil at the beginning of his journey in the larger world may not have differed much from that of Cui and Ma in the past, how that relationship would evolve depended heavily on what transpired in the country over the following decades.

2
The nation

In the old days when educated men ventured beyond their homes into the larger world, they would typically pursue careers in civil service of the universal state. Using the language of theirs, it was to become the emperor's assistant in the noble enterprise of ordering the whole "all-under-heaven." By the 1920s, when the universal state was gone and the "all-under-heaven" world had been invalidated, educated men like Zhang had to set new goals for their careers and find new meanings to their journeys in the world once they left home, even though physically speaking, for most of them the stage on which their life and career evolved was not much different from that of the literati of the imperial period.

That stage was, of course, China. During the second half of the nineteenth century, in the heyday of European and Japanese imperialism, the Qing dynasty lost some territory. For instance, a portion of the Ili River basin in the Central Asian region of Xinjiang was taken by Russia in the 1860s and 1870s, and Taiwan was ceded to Japan in 1895 following the First Sino-Japanese War. However, the majority of its continental empire, including Mongolia, Xinjiang, Tibet, and the so-called China Proper, survived the crisis. This territory was inherited by the Republic of China after the dynasty's collapse and became the home country for educated individuals like Zhang.

Although the territory of the Chinese republic was only slightly smaller than the Qing empire, as a stage of life and career it was of a very different nature. The Republic of China was no longer *the* "central state" but *one of the many* nation-states of the world, now centered in the West. The significance of the careers of people like Zhang would be measured against a bar less of "ordering the world" than of "saving the country," for the Republic of China was one of the weakest states in a brutalized world, and the Chinese nation still faced the challenge of survival.

Many of the concessions made by the Qing to foreign powers through unequal treaties—such as the right of a sovereign state to determine its tariffs and to try foreigners who violated the law on its land—were recognized by the Republic and still stood, constantly reminding the Chinese of their past humiliations and present lack of power. To revise these unequal treaties and regain its sovereignty, China would need a strong state to negotiate with foreign powers, just as Japan did some 30 years before. However, more than a decade into the Republican era, a strong state was exactly what China lacked. The revolution of 1911 that toppled the Qing dynasty avoided widespread bloodshed because a shrewd politician and military strongman of the dynasty, Yuan Shikai, manipulated the situation and persuaded the last emperor to abdicate voluntarily. As a reward, Yuan was allowed to become the provisional president of the new republic, a position originally held by Sun Yat-sen. Sun was willing to focus on more substantial work to rebuild the nation, such as railway construction. However, Yuan's ambition soon overtook him. He became the formal president, then the permanent president, and eventually decided to restore the monarchy and make himself the emperor of a new dynasty. The public was infuriated, and even Yuan's own generals turned against him. In despair and frustration, Yuan died in 1916, and with him, the last chance of maintaining a strong political center was gone.

The young republic entered a stage of political chaos. The central government no longer controlled tax income from the provinces and managed to survive largely through foreign loans. Provinces were controlled by large and small warlords who paid lip service to the central government, jealously guarded their own territories, and frequently fought wars with one another while competing for the opportunity to manipulate the center. This hopeless chaos was the political backdrop of the New Culture Movement and the catalyst for the Nationalist Revolution, which Sun Yat-sen launched during the final years of his life. Unsurprisingly, the two targets of the revolution were the warlords inside the country and imperialism outside.

Like most of his peers, Zhang's career was profoundly shaped by the Nationalist Revolution. Sun Yat-sen's decision to cooperate with the Soviet Union in 1923 injected a strong dose of Leninist rigor into his Nationalist Party (KMT). Party activism, often driven by Communist Party (CCP) members who were now permitted to join the KMT, spread far beyond Guangdong Province in the south, where Sun had set his headquarters. While Zhang was still in middle school, a KMT party organization emerged in Anyang. One of the local organizers, a young woman from a prestigious family that had produced a *jinshi* in the late Qing, was a close friend of Zhang. Zhang himself had been the local leader of the anti-imperialist movement following the May 30th Incident in 1925, a movement that greatly boosted the popularity of the

Nationalist Party. The memoir does not specify exactly when Zhang joined the KMT, but he clearly stated that by the time he left Anyang for Beijing, he was already a member. That membership unexpectedly cut short his studies at Beijing University, yet it also opened a new door for him, leading to a lifelong career path.

As the epicenter of the New Culture Movement and the hub of the country's intellectual life, the atmosphere at Beijing University was fresh and exciting. Here, Zhang was able to see and listen to many of the famous intellectual leaders he had heard about before. There was Liang Qichao of the older generation. There was also Hu Shih of the younger generation who had returned from America and launched the "Literature Revolution" a few years earlier, which quickly replaced classical writing with the vernacular for most people. Given his consistent performance as a student and the positive feedback from his teachers on his coursework, Zhang could have easily earned his degree there, as he initially planned. However, shortly before his studies at Beijing University began, in July 1926, the Nationalist Party officially launched its Northern Expedition from Guangdong to unify the country by military force. Sun Yat-sen had died the previous year, and his protégé Chiang Kai-shek, who had been running the military academy Sun founded with Soviet assistance, became the commander in chief of the National Revolutionary Army, the main force for the military expedition. The warlord from Manchuria, a major target of the expedition, happened to be in control of Beijing and the central government. In response to the revolution from the south, the warlord launched his own wave of terror from Beijing: KMT members were hunted down, rounded up, and executed. In April 1927, one and a half semesters into his study in the foundation program at Beijing University, Zhang managed to secure a reference letter from the local KMT branch and traveled south, with the letter hidden in a secret compartment of his suitcase.

Zhang's plan was to go to Guangzhou, the provincial capital of Guangdong, and apply for the Nationalist Party's military academy, which many of his middle school classmates had enrolled in a couple of years earlier. He traveled along the main railway linking Beijing to the mid-Yangtze River city of Wuhan. After crossing the Yangtze River at Wuhan, he could take another major railway line to Guangzhou. The ongoing war had caused significant damage to the railroads, and at times, he had to disembark, trek to the next station along the railway, and catch a new train to continue his journey. By July, when he arrived in Wuhan, the political situation in the country had changed dramatically. Chiang Kai-shek and the conservative wing of the KMT, resenting the radical labor and peasant movements fueled by the Communist elements of the party, openly broke with the latter, rolled back the Bolshevik influence that Sun had introduced a few years earlier, and turned their swords against their Communist comrades. After a sudden purge that executed thousands of Communists within the KMT, Chiang established a new party headquarters in Nanjing, in the lower Yangtze region, which the Northern Expedition had recently captured from a warlord. The progressive wing of the KMT, still sympathetic to and cooperating with the Communists among them, moved the party headquarters from Guangdong to Wuhan, also recently seized by the expedition forces, and claimed to be the true heirs of Sun's cause. The United Front of the two parties, which had been the source of the youthful energy propelling the Nationalist Revolution, was broken. The Wuhan regime was unsure how far they were willing to go with the Communists. Soon they would turn against them too and "converge" with the Nanjing regime. This convergence would mark the formal end of the United Front and the beginning of the CCP's independent military struggles for political power. However, when Zhang arrived in Wuhan, the political climate was volatile, and the overall situation was unclear.

In Wuhan, Zhang met Guo Shengyong, his best friend and sworn brother from middle school. Guo had graduated from the military academy, become an officer in the National Revolutionary Army, and was now stationed in Wuhan. The two friends stayed in the same room, "put their beds together," and engaged in three nights of discussions about the political situation and Zhang's career prospects. This was the first time ideological commitment intruded into Zhang's personal life. On the fourth day, Zhang concluded that Guo had gone too far to the left and "must have secretly joined the Communist Party." As a result, Zhang left without saying goodbye to his best friend. In his memoir, he justified this decision with the old Confucian saying that "people of different aspirations cannot get along together" and reasoned that this was a case of "sacrificing personal relationships for the sake of public righteousness." Two years later, Guo died after a battle between the two parties and became one of the earliest martyrs for the Communist cause in China.

Zhang, for his part, bought a ship ticket and sailed to Nanjing down the Yangtze River with almost empty pockets. In Nanjing, he was accommodated by a fellow Anyang native who was attending college there. Through recommendations from a former middle school teacher and another fellow Henan native, both with strong KMT connections, Zhang was able to apply to the newly founded Central Party Academy and was admitted in August 1927. Although his study at the party school lasted only one year, it turned out to be a crucial turning point in his career. The school's purpose was to train KMT cadres in political mobilization and propaganda, with Chiang Kai-shek himself serving as its schoolmaster. Here, Zhang forged lifelong connections with top KMT leaders such as Cheng Guofu (1892–1951), the future head of the party's Central Organizational Department. Based on this experience, and in accordance with Chinese tradition, he was able to claim a student–teacher relationship with Chiang Kai-shek, just like the hundreds of graduates from the military academy where Chiang was also the schoolmaster. Zhang would eventually become a professor at this academy after earning a degree in America, and spent decades teaching at the institution until his retirement.

In June 1928, Zhang graduated from the academy, ranking at the top of his class. His "internship" involved political work in the National Revolutionary Army during the final stage of the Northern Expedition, in which the KMT extended its victories all the way into Beijing and formally reunified the country. However, the new national government Chiang Kai-shek established in Nanjing was more of a central authority in name than in reality, as many warlords were co-opted instead of being defeated and destroyed by the KMT, and hence retained much autonomy. The government could exercise effective control only over several provinces in the lower Yangtze. Genuine political integration was a long way off, let alone social transformation and industrialization. Nonetheless, this was a significant milestone in Sun Yat-sen's vision for the long-term national rejuvenation of China. In the following decade, the KMT would struggle to govern, modernize, and transform China amid numerous distractions until the outbreak of the Second Sino-Japanese War in 1937 completely disrupted its efforts. Many people refer to this period as the "Golden Decade" of the Republic of China, though many of the KMT regime's weaknesses and limitations were also exposed during this time.

Zhang volunteered—and was approved—to be sent to Xinjiang to establish a new party branch in the frontier region. However, the project was aborted due to the local military leader's objections, as it would enhance the central government's control. Zhang ended up working for the KMT's Central Department of Organization briefly, and then in the party bureaucracies of several heartland provinces. As a capable young man, he had no trouble handling his responsibilities effectively. However, the KMT, now that it had become the ruling party, quickly shed the spartan spirit characteristic of a revolutionary organization and became plagued by cronyism and nepotism, like other regimes with unchecked power. Zhang was likely too proud to engage in the corrupt practices he looked down upon. Yet, as a party official, he personally witnessed the superficiality and decadence that permeated both life and work within the party bureaucracy. He wrote about the complacency and clichés evident in the banquets that provincial party officials organized to entertain inspectors sent from the center. His anxiety over this moral decline may have contributed to his desire to further his studies overseas, though it was likely not the sole or most important factor, as he himself appeared adept in social situations and often benefited from his social skills.

There was a deeper motive behind Zhang's ambitions. He had been seeking such opportunities long before entering the party bureaucracy. In 1926, while working as the magistrate's communication assistant in Anyang and before enrolling at Beijing University, he used his connections in the local government to reach out to the foreign manager of the Liuhegou mining company (located within the jurisdiction of Anyang County) to explore the possibility of studying in the US. (It is unclear whether the manager was actually from the US.; it is possible that a young admirer of Western civilization in an inland northern Chinese county did not recognize the differences between Western countries.) That effort did not yield any results, but he seemed determined to pursue his studies in the US. In 1929, he petitioned Chiang Kai-shek, through Chen Guofu, for a study abroad opportunity in the US under the patronage of the Central Political Academy (Figure 2). This effort "did not bear fruit" either, as he noted. Then, in 1931, upon learning about the competition for Henan Province's governmental fund to study abroad, he left his promising career in the party bureaucracy and took the examination for that opportunity. It was evident that for Zhang, the nationalist, the center of the world was in the West, and that to better serve his nationalist ideals, a journey to the West, the training there, and advanced knowledge from there, were all essential.

He won the opportunity and studied for three and a half years at Stanford University between October 1931 and March 1935, earning a BA and an MA in political science (Figure 3). By that point, he was as clear as in 1931 when he decided to study in

Figure 2 Zhang Jinjian at the GMT Central Political Academy, 1928. (Source: *Zhang Jinjian jiaoshou jinian wenji*.)

the US, that his life and career were all back home in China. He consulted with his adviser at Stanford, Angell Cottrell, regarding career prospects in China and took Cottrell's advice to position himself at the intersection of party bureaucracy and academia. The vast majority of his life after returning to China was spent as a professor at the KMT Central Party Academy. He made his name as the founder of public administration studies in China. In this role, he essentially introduced what he had learned in the US to China, applying the methods and theories he had acquired on Chinese contexts.

Commercial Press Salary Scale (c. 1912–27)		
Education	Monthly Salary (Ch$)	Perquisites
Chinese College (with experience)	80	3′ × 1½′

Commercial Press Salary Scale (c. 1912–27)		
Japanese College	100–120	3´ × 2´ desk
Japanese Imperial University	150	4´ × 2½´ desk; bookshelf; crystal ink stand; and rattan chair
Western College	200	same as the preceding
Harvard. Yale, Oxford, or Cambridge	250	custom-made desk; bookshelf; crystal ink stand; and rattan chair

Source: Y.C. Wang, Chinese Intellectuals and the West, 1872–1949 (Chapel Hill: University of North Carolina Press, 1966), p. 90.

Zhang's admiration of modern Western civilization, and the determination to see his own country catch up was common among nationalists in the non-West countries at the turn of the twentieth century. Compared with Cui's comfortable sense of superiority over the "barbarians," and Ma's threatened sense of superiority and efforts to maintain a resemblance of parity, Zhang's view of

Figure 3 The passport photo of Zhang Jinjian, prior to his trip to the US, 1931. (Source: *Zhang Jinjian jiaoshou jinian wenji*.)

China's position in the world was a clear indication that for the educated Chinese of the twentieth century, the sense of "centrality" was completely gone. However, in Zhang's case, as in the case of most modern Chinese intellectuals, there is no sign of "subjectivity loss" and of "mimicry" of the whites.[8] He was securely a Chinese despite all the admiration of Western civilization and the humiliations China had endured recently.

One interesting sign of this is that Zhang wrote classical-style Chinese poems after his visit to a strip bar in California to mark the exotic experience, a typical and almost ritualized practice for the literati on unusual occasions. In his memoir, he said relatively little about his life in the US except for the hard work he put into his courses and the cities he visited as a tourist. His view of the people in the US is positive, and his experiences in the country were generally pleasant. However, there was no particular excitement in his tone when he wrote about these. Upon reflecting on his life at age 70, what came to his mind was almost completely a life that had evolved in China. Yet he wrote several books introducing US political thought and institutions, and political theories of the West in general. The West, and the US in particular, stood out as a world set apart and above. China was his own country, where his life evolved and in which he was actively engaged. He seemed comfortable living in and discussing this country of his own. It mattered little that his country might be just an insignificant corner in the grand scheme of things.

Upon returning to China, Zhang became a sought-after asset. A salary scale from Commercial Press—one of the most influential publishers during the Republican era—illustrates that students who had returned, particularly those with degrees from prestigious US universities, were paid up to three times more than their peers with comparable degrees from domestic institutions, and they enjoyed various benefits associated with an elevated status (Figure 4). Although he still needed to enter the job market, his credentials, background, and connections made the process much easier. With recommendations from Chen Guofu, Zhang quickly received offers and explored several positions, including one in the KMT's Central Department of Organization and another as the editor in chief of a regional newspaper in the northwestern province of Gansu.

By August 1935, less than half a year after graduating from Stanford, he accepted a professorship at Henan University, one of the country's eight national universities located in Kaifeng, the capital of Henan Province. This decision was partly motivated by his duty to serve his home province, as his study in America was funded by Henan Province's public resources, and the chief of the province's Department of Education had written to urge him to take this path. This marked the beginning of his teaching career, which would become his primary engagement for the rest of his life. All the political and administrative activities he would later undertake were conducted in the capacity of a professor.

As a scholar, Zhang was both diligent and prolific. Throughout his career, he published more than 40 books. His first book, a general introduction to the theories and practices of public administration that he studied at Stanford, was published almost immediately upon his return to China. This book was widely adopted as a university-level textbook and earned him considerable fame. Shortly after he began teaching at Henan University, both the prestigious Nankai University and Beijing University invited him to join their faculties.

Commercial Press Salary Scale (c. 1912–27)

Education	Monthly Salary (Ch$)	Perquisites
Chinese College (with experience)	80	3' × 1½' desk
Japanese College	100–120	3' × 2' desk
Japanese Imperial University	150	4' × 2½' desk; book shelf; crystal ink stand; and rattan chair
Western College	200	same as the preceding
Harvard, Yale, Oxford, or Cambridge	250	custom-made desk; book shelf; crystal ink stand; and rattan chair

Source: Y. C. Wang, *Chinese Intellectuals and the West, 1872–1949* (Chapel Hill: University of North Carolina Press, 1966), p. 90.

Figure 4 Commerce Press's pay scale (Source, Lloyd Eastman, *Family, Field, and Ancestors: Constancy and Change in China's Social and Economic History, 1550–1949*, Oxford University Press, 1988 p. 202.)

Now, as a rising star in academia, Zhang faced a potential dilemma: he was torn between his ambition to advance his career and his sense of duty to serve his home province. Ironically, it was the precarious political situation that led him to a satisfactory solution. The invitation letter from Beijing University, which would have been harder to resist, was sent to the wrong address and never reached him. He did receive the letter from Nankai and initially declined the invitation. However, the university insisted; its founder, the nationally reputable and highly respected Zhang Boling, personally invited him during a face-to-face meeting. Meanwhile, Zhang's political activism as a professor at Henan University had recently caused an incident that resulted in his imprisonment for a month. Staying at Henan University could have been controversial. Therefore, Zhang accepted a position as a professor at Nankai University in Tianjin in June 1936.

The incident that led to Zhang's predicament at Henan University involved a voluntary association he organized for students in the fall of 1935, called the League of Loyal and Righteous Youth. This patriotic society aimed to allow students to express their commitment to resisting Japanese aggression and to exert pressure on the government to prioritize defense policies against this threat. Several years earlier, on September 18, 1931—the day Zhang sailed to America for his studies—Japan suddenly attacked and occupied Manchuria, a fully integrated Chinese territory at the time. Over the following years, Japan continued encroaching toward China proper. By 1935, the Japanese military had reached the vicinity of Beijing, and its political influence forced Chiang Kai-shek's National Government in Nanjing to accept high degrees of autonomy in parts of northern China.

The public sentiment was clear: citizens wanted the government to halt its efforts against the Communist rebels in the south and focus instead on the foreign invasion in the north. However, this popular opinion carried significant political consequences. The two major political parties, the KMT and the CCP, each operated under their own partisan logic. Chiang Kai-shek refused to confront the much stronger Japanese forces until he could eradicate the Communists, whom he viewed as a "disease in the inner organ" compared to the Japanese aggression he considered merely a "nuisance at the skin level." Meanwhile, the CCP, with their base areas in the southern provinces facing tremendous military pressure from Chiang, skillfully redirected public anger at the government's failure in national defense toward him by proposing an end to the civil war and the formation of a new United Front against the Japanese.

The Chinese nation was thus a house divided against itself, unable to withstand external aggression. Since Chiang Kai-shek decided that some territorial loss, albeit temporary, was a necessary price to pay for consolidation within the country, he was determined to endure public pressure and take a hard-line stance against the Communists. In such circumstances, the seemingly innocent and innocuous activities of patriotism suddenly became sensitive political declarations. The youth league that Zhang founded soon attracted the attention of the Henan branch of the Blue Shirts, Chiang's secret police.

Zhang's motives for this initiative were somewhat complicated. In addition to serving as a professor, he was also director of the Office of Student Conduct, making it fully legitimate for him to establish an organization to guide student patriotic activities. However, he also admitted that another part of him hoped the organization could build his influence in Henan and lay the groundwork for future political advancement. Despite his mixed motivations, this move as a political action was somewhat hasty. He was reported to the Blue Shirts for allegedly violating paperwork procedures, subsequently abducted, brought to Nanjing, and imprisoned in a military jail for a month in the spring of 1936. On the way to the jail, he feared he would be secretly executed, as such cursory executions were common at the time for political prisoners.

Back in Henan, the sudden disappearance of a professor caused a scandal. With the intervention of Chen Guofu, Zhang was released, and the head of the Blue Shirts blamed the provincial branch for the "mistake." Infuriated, Zhang considered directly appealing to Chiang Kai-shek to seek retribution for the offense.

However, Chen stopped him, making it clear that organizing the youth league without first consulting Chiang and himself was a gross misstep. This incident marked Zhang's first foray into political action. In his mid-30s, he was still relatively inexperienced as a politician, even though he was only a part-time one. He would learn from this experience and become a more careful planner in his later engagements. Nevertheless, his position as a patriotic nationalist was clearly demonstrated in the "missteps" of this event. Given his experience as a party operative and his skills in cultivating good rapport with his mentors, his failure to consult with Chen and Chiang before founding the youth league can only be explained by his simple and unquestionable belief that there could be nothing wrong with patriotism. Like many modern Chinese intellectuals, Zhang's patriotism seemed to be an inherited cultural gene. For the modern counterparts of the late imperial "assistants of the emperor," the nation became the rightful object of loyalty now that the monarch had gone, and patriotic intellectuals became the "avatars" of the upright literati of old.

Zhang's other significant extra-professorial engagement can also be understood in the context of a patriotic intellectual seeking to concretely transform the country, often utilizing what he learned in the West. This refers to his involvement in the Rural Reconstruction Movement shortly after he joined Nankai University. The Rural Reconstruction Movement consisted of various efforts aimed at revitalizing the dilapidated rural society through patient and moderate reform programs. It was championed by returned students such as the Yale-educated Jame Yen (1890–1990) and the Columbia-educated Tao Xingzhi

(1891–1946), as well as domestically trained scholars like the Beijing University philosopher Liang Shuming (1893–1988). Faced with the violent land reform and class warfare propagated by the CCP on one hand, and the KMT's neglect of rural decay and peasant suffering on the other, this approach was quiet yet possibly the only viable way to modernize the country's vast and impoverished rural society. Specific programs, including mass literacy, disease control, improvements in rural administration, basic modern agronomy and husbandry knowledge for peasants, and the development of village industries, were eventually adopted by governments in both Taiwan and mainland China once the political turmoil had subsided.

In July 1936, several leading universities in the country collaborated with prominent rural reconstruction institutions on a project to implement their programs in selected counties in northern China. Zhang, representing Nankai University, participated in a program aimed at enhancing rural administration. He brought graduate students to the field in Jining County, Shandong Province, where he was temporarily appointed as a county official. There, they successfully conducted a county-wide land cadastral survey and streamlined the county's land tax collection procedures.

When some county government clerks attempted to continue the abuses of the past by embezzling collected tax funds, Zhang resolutely enforced discipline in the traditional manner, having them beaten with bamboo sticks in the county court. Given that Zhang's MA thesis at Stanford focused on US municipal governance and that part of his research in China was centered on local governance, his participation in the program in Jining

County exemplifies the practical application of modern professional knowledge to address specific rural challenges in China. Whether or not knowledge of US municipal governance proved useful for enhancing administrative efficiency in rural northern China, having a well-trained political scientist with considerable social and political skills engage in rural governance issues was undoubtedly a promising step for a modernizing country.

The program in Jining was left unfinished as the outbreak of full-scale war with Japan altered its course. In fact, the war changed everything in China. Prior to this, in December 1936, a Manchurian warlord—the son of the warlord whose reign of terror in Beijing a decade earlier had forced Zhang to leave—who had joined Chiang Kai-shek at the end of the Northern Expedition and served as his deputy, grew disillusioned with Chiang's "fight the Communists first" strategy. He kidnapped Chiang while the leader was on an inspection tour in the northwest, where the warlord was stationed after the loss of his home base in Manchuria. He deemed his actions "militarily advising" the leader.

With his life at risk, Chiang agreed to alter his policy and cease hostilities against the Communists. This incident marked one of the most dramatic turning points in the country's modern history. Chiang's plan to exterminate the CCP was nearly accomplished; he had driven them from their base areas in the south, chased them into the impoverished and sparsely populated region around a town called Yan'an in the northwestern highlands, and surrounded them with heavy military forces. One more decisive blow could have completed the job. But the Manchurian warlord, with his ancestral home occupied by the Japanese, grew sympathetic to the Communist proposal day by day. When he suddenly pulled the trigger, the course of the country was switched in a direction nobody could have foreseen.

Chiang kept his promise, and the Communists got the desperately needed breathing space they sought. When a new round of Japanese aggression occurred in a suburb of Beijing in July 1937, Chiang did not order Chinese troops to refrain from fighting back. What began as a minor skirmish quickly escalated into total war between the two countries, spreading across the entire East Asian continent. Japan swiftly occupied Beijing and advanced south along the railway lines. Within less than two months, they had come alarmingly close to Jining. Recognizing the impending threat, Zhang sent his wife—who was now five months pregnant with their first child—back to Anyang while he remained until the last possible moment. He then led the students and other faculty members from the program in a southward retreat.

Zhang's wife was accompanied by his maternal uncle, who was living with them in Jining. They arrived home only to find that Anyang was also on the verge of falling to the Japanese. Zhang's father decided to lead the family south to meet Zhang in Suiping, a county in southern Henan located 200 miles from Anyang, where Zhang's program had planned to relocate and continue their work. By the end of the year, Zhang's team finally arrived in Suiping, but his family was no longer there. Relatives from Anyang sent messages to Zhang's father, alerting him that local bullies were trying to take advantage of the chaos to loot their family home. In response, the elder Zhang resolved to return and settle these issues first. As a result, Zhang's son was born in Anyang under Japanese occupation the following spring. Meanwhile, Zhang and his team, realizing that Suiping was also not a safe enough location for the program, decided to move farther south. They eventually settled in the southwestern province of Guizhou, closer to the wartime capital at Chongqing.

Massive displacement, similar to what Zhang's team and family experienced, became a daily reality for the country during the war. Following several large battles, China fragmented into multiple regions. The Japanese occupied the eastern (and more developed) half of the country, including all the major cities and railway lines. Chiang Kai-shek relocated what remained of his military, along with the government, essential machinery, and key personnel, to the mountainous southwest, establishing Chongqing as the temporary capital. There, leveraging the region's topography and counting on Japan's lack of resources to conquer such a vast territory as China, he barely survived but stubbornly refused to surrender. The CCP, recognizing Chiang's authority while insisting on an "independent effort" to fight the Japanese, took root in the northwest, making Yan'an its headquarters. They initiated guerrilla warfare behind Japanese lines by mobilizing peasants whom Japan had conquered but could not control. Amid tremendous hardship and danger, millions of people migrated from the eastern regions to the western part of the country and from cities to rural areas. Some followed Chiang's government to Chongqing and the southwest, while others—particularly educated youth—were inspired by the CCP's idealistic vision and puritanical spirit to trek to Yan'an. Many more, however, simply could not bear to live under the humiliating and often brutal rule of the Japanese and relocated to areas that were not occupied by Japan (Figure 5).

Beneath and behind such large-scale human migration and the trials of war, however, was the quiet transformation of China's nationalism. By the beginning of the war, nationalism was still predominantly an urban and intellectual sentiment. It was primarily the urban and educated population who were informed and talked about issues at the national level, who felt that the country—not just the immediate environment of their lives—was theirs, and who identified with the nation. With the movement and mingling of people, particularly in response to Japanese atrocities in both cities and the countryside, the concept of a "nation" was rapidly felt and embraced by all, leading peasants to join the nationalist cause. A pair of posters depicting the changing face of the war—before and after the outbreak of total war—vividly illustrated this shift, highlighting how peasants became the main fighters against the Japanese (Figures 6 and 7). Thus, China's war with Japan evolved into a genuine national war of resistance. Such a war would prove impossible for Japan to win. After Pearl Harbor, with the US joining the fight, it was only a matter of time before Japan would be defeated.

By August 1938, Zhang's rural reconstruction program in Guizhou was completed, and his initial contract with Nankai University was about to expire. The KMT Central Party Academy, now relocated to Chongqing, extended an invitation for him to return and teach. Zhang happily accepted and resettled in Chongqing. About a year later, his parents decided to bring his wife and baby son out of Japanese-occupied Anyang to join him. His uncle was able to accompany and assist them once again. Over the course of two months, the group of five trekked thousands of miles, traversing territories controlled by both the Japanese and

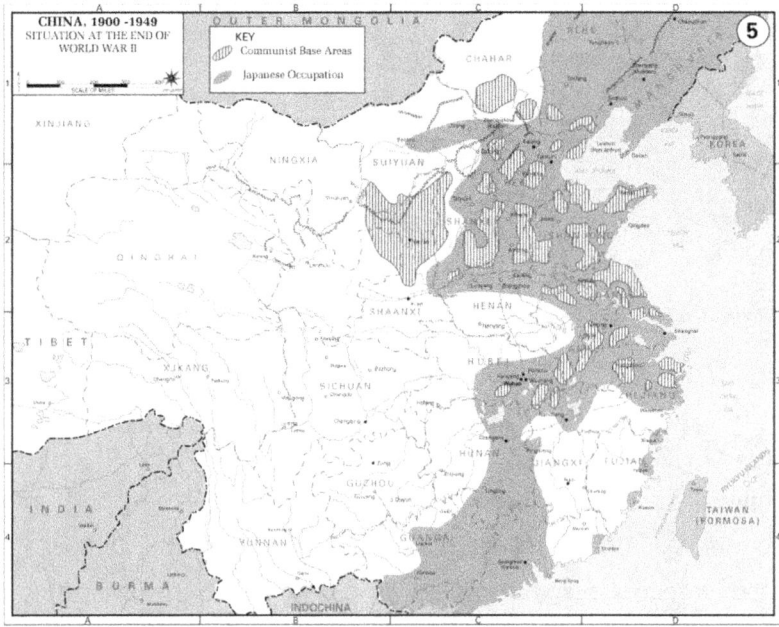

Figure 5 World War II situation in China. (Source: https://www.pacificatrocities.org/blog/how-much-of-china-did-japan-control-at-its-greatest-extent)

the Communists, and finally reunited with Zhang in Chongqing. They remained together until 1946 when the capital was moved back to Nanjing after the war ended. During this time, his wife gave birth to three daughters, while Zhang himself gained more influence and established broader connections as a politically active scholar and a specialist adviser to various governmental programs during the war years.

In December 1944, Zhang was ready to make another commitment and become involved in political affairs again. This time, his plan was to get elected to the National Political Consultation Assembly from Henan. Although the assembly was still an

Figure 6 (upper) and **Figure 7** (lower): Fighters against Japan in China from the early 1930s to the late 1930s. Note the typical fighter for the nation changed from urban intellectuals to peasants. (Source: Henrietta Harrison, *China*, Oxford University Press, 2001)

advisory body rather than a legislative one, it served as a prototype for a national congress before the establishment of formal constitutional governance in China. Many influential figures were interested in it and were competing for positions. Chen Guofu supported Zhang's campaign by appointing him as the special inspector of Henan Province's party affairs, representing the KMT's Central Department of Organization. Back in Henan, where the provincial capital had temporarily relocated to areas not occupied by the Japanese, Zhang mobilized his old friends, classmates, teachers, and students to run a brief but successful campaign. By the time the new session of the assembly opened in May 1945 in Chongqing, the war was coming to an end, and Zhang was eager to engage in significant endeavors—like many others—both for the sake of his country and for his own aspirations.

Nationalism is arguably the most important theme of China throughout the twentieth century. In a sense, all the educated class were nationalists. But there were diverse visions of what the nation needed, where it should go, and even who constituted the Chinese nation. Liberals like Hu Shih, bearing influence from Anglo-American liberalism, urged their fellow Chinese to engage in rational thinking and aspire to become dignified individuals, before China could advance to the level of these developed countries. In contrast, Communists like Mao and his comrades, influenced by the Soviet Union, viewed China as a "proletariat nation" within a world defined by antagonism between the oppressors and the oppressed. From this perspective, national salvation required class warfare in which "the people" would expel the international bourgeoisie from China and eliminate their domestic allies—namely, the landlords, the reactionary government, and the crony capitalists who supported and benefited from the state. As a proletariat nation, China would eventually unite with the world's proletariats and strive to become their leader.

Zhang's nationalism was more aligned with that of cultural conservatives, emphasizing Chinese tradition in defining the modern Chinese nation. While they recognized the strengths of other countries, they insisted that China must find its own path rather than simply emulate the models of other nations, be it the US or Russia. Much of this tradition was rooted in Confucianism, but in this context, Confucianism was no longer treated as a universal culture; it was seen as a unique tradition belonging to the Chinese people. In modern times, this made China not "central" but distinct.

In 1935, shortly before Zhang's return from the US, the cultural conservatives' stance on nationalism was proclaimed in a call for "China-based cultural reconstruction" by ten nationally renowned professors. One of the co-signers, Sa Mengwu, later became a close friend of Zhang. Another, Tao Xisheng, elaborated on their positions in the book he coauthored with Chiang Kai-shek in 1943, titled *China's Destiny*. By that time, the most difficult days of the war were behind them, and Chiang was looking forward to postwar national reconstruction. Britain and the US had relinquished all the treaty privileges they had gained from China during the Qing dynasty, now that China was an ally in the war against Japan. Things appeared hopeful. With China being treated as an equal by the major powers and on the verge of liberation from one of the worst foreign invasions in modern history, it seemed possible that China could stand in peace with other nations, embracing a cultural tradition that, while no longer as glamorous as it once was, was nonetheless comfortably its own.

3
The home place

The very first line of Zhang's memoir states that "the country is a collection of home places." The first chapter, which is on his home place, is divided into two sections: the first section on Anyang County, the second on his home village Xiahan. Zhang's opening statement regarding the relationship between polity and locality closely echoes the views of the literati from earlier times. As the philosopher Wang Yangming of the Ming dynasty expressed, "the grandeur of the 'all-under-heaven' is a collection of local places." Although the term "all-under-heaven" has now been supplanted by the less universal term "country," the aggregate view of polity remains the same, with local places serving as the building blocks of the whole.

Traditional Chinese society operated within a hierarchy of places, all originally defined as administrative entities, such as the county, the prefecture, the province. At the top was the "all-under-heaven," which sometimes embraced things outside of the central state (*zhongguo*), but in common usage was coterminous with the central state, and in any case included most of the known world.[9] Within this hierarchical structure, individuals could identify with any level or levels as "home," depending on the specific circumstances of the time, place, and person. Most literati had their local identities crystallized at the county and/

or prefectural level, largely because this was where their careers began, specifically with the local-level civil service examinations, and it represented the most significant initial stage of their social lives. In the case of Anyang, the identities of the county and the prefecture often merged, as Anyang County served as the primary county of Zhangde Prefecture. The predominant part of a place often tends to perceive itself as the whole. Thus, in the old days, when Cui and Ma engaged in local affairs, they referred to either Zhangde Prefecture or Anyang County, depending on the context. However, the prefecture was abolished as an administrative level at the beginning of the Republican era, and the name "Zhangde," which had been in use for over 800 years, was retired in the twentieth century. By the time Zhang's generation emerged, the home place that was larger than the immediate village environment—but not so large that it felt unfamiliar—was clearly identified as Anyang County.

The profound changes that befell China during the several decades before Zhang was born can be summarized as the decline and fall of its "all-under-heaven" world, and the evaporation of its universal state (the "central state"). But such change concerned mostly China's position in the larger world. One may call it the collapse of China's "world order." Inside China, the "order of places" remained intact. Localities retained their position—and irreducible dignity—as the building blocks of the whole, though that whole was by now not *the* universal state but just *a* nation-state. If anything, their status was more elevated.

During the decades of crisis of the polity, the last generations of the literati statesmen repeatedly resorted to the ancient political wisdom of reinvigorating the local parts to strengthen the polity as a whole. Such strategy, if one follows their aggregate view of the polity, is almost intuitive. As Wang Yangming stated, immediately after the phrase quoted above, "if all the counties and prefectures are put in good order whole "all-under-heaven" will be in good order."[10]

Beginning from the earliest reform movement of the Qing in the 1860s to the late Qing reforms in the 1900s, there was a constant call on the court to "broaden the channel of communication" with local gentry, and on the latter to participate more in reinvigorating local societies. Initially, these calls emerged from the center's perspective and aimed to "mobilize" societal energy to save the state. However, as the local gentry became increasingly involved in public and political affairs and as the dynasty faced deepening crises, it inevitably became apparent that this meant granting the local gentry more power. This shift represented a transition from being simply administered by court-appointed local officials to allowing them to "govern themselves." In 1905, the Qing court issued decrees to establish institutions of local self-governance across provinces, prefectures, counties, and even districts below the county level. Although the councils and assemblies established during the last years of the Qing were not fully developed legislative bodies, their share of power was steadily increasing.

So, "the local" loomed large as China entered the twentieth century. Local self-governance became one of the most commonly accepted themes of political life during the first decade of the Republic. Training schools for local self-governance were established by both the central government and various provincial governments. Sun Yat-sen was a strong advocate of this concept, envisioning the county as the basic self-governing unit and a training ground for implementing formal nationwide constitutional rule once his military reunification efforts were achieved. Others, including some warlords, were more focused on practicing local self-governance at the provincial level. By the early 1920s, this interest contributed to the Provincial Constitution Movement, which advocated for a future of united self-governing provinces in China. Mao Zedong was a dedicated participant in this movement in his home province of Hunan, where he envisioned a "Republic of Hunan" leading the charge to save China, starting at the provincial level.

Zhang's Henan Province was not particularly active in the push for a provincial constitution. However, county-level self-governance councils had been established since the late Qing dynasty, and these councils continued to function throughout the Republican era, with only a brief interruption during Yuan Shikai's rule. In Anyang, the last president of the county council was Zhang's middle school physics teacher, Zhang Tianji, who became the school's headmaster shortly after Zhang's graduation in 1925.

In such circumstances, it is natural that much of the localist orientation of the literati carried over into the Republican era. While many found it challenging to feel comfortable in the new world or make sense of the newly conceptualized nation, the educated class found it relatively easy to connect with their home localities. They could engage more actively in local public affairs if they stayed home or assist their communities from afar. For one thing, the local area was where many people placed their hopes for the future. Additionally, amid the rapid pace of change during that time, the local provided a sense of continuity. This explains the flourishing of the millennium-old practice of compiling and publishing local gazetteers during the Republican era.

The local gazetteer was the most common genre of writings about places in traditional China. All levels of administrative divisions, from the county to the universal state, had their gazetteers, which were often periodically updated to reflect local conditions. These gazetteers recorded the history and geography of the areas, as well as key social and economic data such as landholdings, taxation quotas, names of degree holders, and lists of local officials. Typically, a gazetteer was compiled by local literati, although the local magistrate often served as the organizer. It was common for the most celebrated literatus of a locality to preside over the gazetteer project during his retirement or even prior to that. For example, Cui Xian wrote the Zhangde Prefectural gazetteer during the Ming dynasty while on a break between two official appointments. The audience for these gazetteers included higher-level authorities, who required information from below, but they were increasingly aimed at the local community itself. In fact, most gazetteers were initiated from within local regions and were read more frequently by the local literati. In this sense, the local gazetteer represented a genre created for the local and by the local.

At present, there are about 8,000 local gazetteers extant from the Sung through the Qing dynasty. Against this background, the Republican period produced more than 1,600 titles of local gazetteers during a short period of 38 years up until the Communist takeover in 1949.[11] Even taking into consideration the factor of non-extant titles in the past, the Republican era was by far the most productive period for the local gazetteer. Beneath the flourishing of the gazetteer genre, one can hardly miss the burst of vitality surrounding its subject—the locality: people grew more enthusiastic in writing and reading about their home places during the Republican era because they were more concerned with and more engaged in their local communities.

The Anyang County gazetteer of 1933 is one of the most highly praised Republican gazetteers for its quality. The process of its compilation and publication reflects the enthusiasm and dedication that local elites in Anyang had for their home place. The project began in 1921, prompted by a call from the provincial government. Since the previous edition of the county's gazetteer had been compiled more than a century earlier, in 1820, the local gentry was highly supportive of creating a new one. A "county gazetteer bureau" was established specifically for this purpose, with a local gentleman appointed as the bureau head and funding provided by the county's public budget. The first draft of the new gazetteer was nearly complete when it was disrupted by regional wars between warlords. The bureau's physical location was requisitioned by troops of one warlord who occupied the county seat, resulting in the loss of completed chapters—some on paper and others already inscribed into woodblocks and ready for printing—in the ensuing chaos. Subsequently, three more local gentlemen took on the role of bureau head in attempts to restart the project, but all efforts failed to materialize due to the ongoing conflicts.

After the KMT reunification, the project was reopened in the spring of 1931 through a renewed initiative by the local gentry and approval from one of the county magistrate's formal executive conferences. This time, it was under the leadership of the fifth head of the bureau, and the new draft was finally completed in the fall of 1933. The acknowledgments page features a list of "helpers" involved in the project, which reads like a roll call of the elite members of county society. This includes the district heads from all ten districts of the county and the chairs of the peasants' association and the chamber of commerce, as well as prominent Anyang natives residing elsewhere. Once the draft was finalized, it was taken to the provincial capital, Kaifeng, where a group of Anyang sojourners working in various provincial-level institutions—presumably with higher cultural credentials—spent a month editing and revising it.

Instead of the traditional woodblock printing that had been used for centuries in Chinese publishing, the final production of the gazetteer utilized a new technology: the finalized draft was sent to Beijing for lithographic printing, which was steadily becoming the new standard. A series of other innovations were also incorporated into the new gazetteer, like those found in many other local gazetteers of the Republican era. These included new cartographic technologies for mapping the county and the addition of new categories of information to reflect changes in social realities, such as the newly established self-governance institutions, modern industries, and transportation facilities.

Despite these innovations, the narrative style was deliberately designed to demonstrate continuity with previous gazetteers regarding the recording of various issues. For example, the chapter on degree holders from the old examination system was retained and supplemented with names of graduates from modern universities and vocational schools, as well as elected officials at various levels of local assemblies. The purpose of such arrangement was to "conform to the conventional ideal of selecting the best from the local societies to fill positions of power and authority." In the statement on compilation styles that prefaces the gazetteer, the editors made it clear that they viewed their project as a continuation of all previous gazetteer efforts. They aimed to make the current edition "connectable and compatible" with earlier editions so that they could ultimately be regarded as "one book."

The head of the gazetteer bureau who oversaw its completion was an old-style Confucian scholar with a profound awareness that the civilization he grew up in was being replaced by a new one. This sensitivity instilled in him a sense of urgency to undertake the gazetteer project, as he recognized that "older people who were learned [about the past]" were quickly fading away. Therefore, the gazetteer needed to be completed before they all died off. Yet, the almost seamless integration of the old and the new in the gazetteer produced under his leadership suggests that it was the locality that underwent China's modern transformation most steadily and successfully.

Zhang was not involved in the gazetteer project, mostly because his career had taken him too far away from home. When the final and most crucial stage of the gazetteer project started in the spring of 1931, he was already set for studying in the US, and soon left the country in the fall. When he came back in 1935, the project had long since been completed. Had he remained nearby and been needed, he surely would have participated. One of his friends, the journalist Zhang Liaoqie who was then working for the Tianjin-based newspaper *Ta Kung Pao* and was stationed in Kaifeng, was part of the team that did the final editing of the gazetteer. For his own part, Zhang had never severed connections with his home place ever since his career pursuit led him away from Anyang. He visited home whenever he had the chance, and all money he managed to save from his salary as a professor, he sent home so that his father could build up the family farm. Throughout his career, Zhang had always been eager to do something for his home place, whether the home village or the county.

In the summer of 1928, shortly after graduating from the Central Political Academy and just before reporting to his new position in the GMD Central Department of Organization, Zhang made a brief visit home. The Nationalist Revolution had recently succeeded in reunifying the country, and the mood of revolutionary triumph was at its peak. Riding the wave of this momentum, a movement to "turn temples into schools" spread swiftly across the land. The logic behind this movement was simple: the hundreds of thousands of local temples represented the most concrete embodiment of past superstitions and were seen as direct obstacles to enlightening the people and modernizing the country. Meanwhile, modern elementary schools were recognized as the most effective means to achieve these goals, yet they were severely undersupplied at the time. Thus, what could be more beneficial to the nationalist cause than closing these temples, destroying the icons, and converting the spaces into schools? As a young man poised to embark on a promising career in the revolutionary party that had just seized political power, Zhang quickly saw an opportunity to help revolutionize and modernize his home village.

In his home village of Xiahan, there was an Earth God temple that housed a statue of the Anyang City God in the main hall, while the wing rooms were dedicated to statues of ghosts from the underworld. As a child, Zhang had always been frightened by the fearsome expressions of the ghosts. Now, he felt it was time to eradicate them. He consulted with his family and secured the support of his father, who had once served as the district head and was influential among the local gentry. With the help of his younger brother Jinxi, who directed the hired laborers, they dug a large pit in the courtyard of the temple and buried all the statues overnight. On the temple site, they founded the "Invigorating China National Elementary School," which became the first new-style school in the district. Part of the school's funding came from selling off the hundreds of old cypress trees from another village temple. Zhang also donated a complete set of "elementary student readers" published by the Commercial Press in Shanghai as textbooks. From a twenty-first-century perspective, Zhang's iconoclastic actions—especially the sale of the old trees from an ancient temple—might appear overly radical. However, the young revolutionary felt triumphant. In his memoir, he recounted an encounter on the road with an elderly woman who used to visit the temple to pray to the gods. She told him that the man who had destroyed the temple had been punished by the gods with a sudden stroke and was now lying in bed, waiting to die. Zhang burst out laughing and proudly declared, "I am the guy who destroyed the god statues!"

In the summer of 1931, before departing for his studies in the US, Zhang made another visit home to Anyang. With his recent experiences in the KMT party system, he had clearly become someone the local community turned to for assistance. Shortly after his arrival, the leaders of Xiahan village sent a small delegation to visit Zhang at his family home. The purpose of their visit was to formally invite him to lead an irrigation project they had been contemplating for some time.

Xiahan village is located at a midpoint between two rivers: the Zhang River to the north and the Anyang River to the south. Villages along both rivers had enjoyed the benefits of ancient irrigation channels fed by these waterways. However, Xiahan's relatively distant location from both rivers forced its residents to rely on wells when precipitation fell short for their crops. Villagers in Xiahan envied the easy and reliable irrigation water available to other villages and had long dreamed of constructing a separate canal to draw water from the Anyang River to the south. Yet, this ambitious project was too daunting for them to undertake alone. It would require navigating complex negotiations with neighboring villages along the river, securing permission from the government, raising funds from the village community, and, of course, managing the intricate work of actual construction. Ultimately, all these challenges boiled down to the need for strong and capable leadership to bring their vision to fruition.

Immediately accepting the invitation, Zhang's organizational skills and connections in the outside world were on full display in the project. He gave the proposed canal an appealing name, "Grand Harmony," reflecting its purpose of sharing water with neighboring villages. A committee was quickly formed to oversee the initiative, and Zhang's father was elected as the designated person to manage the engineering aspects of the project. The costs were shared among all villagers based on the size of their farms, while local commercial firms contributed donations proportional to the scale of their businesses. Xiahan, being of considerable size and functioning as a local market town, hosted several cotton and grain wholesale businesses. The funding issue was resolved swiftly. Ground-level surveying and mapping were entrusted to a hired specialist. The most challenging aspect of the project was petitioning the county and provincial governments for a permit and persuading the villages along the Anyang River—who had been benefiting from the existing irrigation canal—to agree to share water. Zhang successfully navigated these challenges by leveraging his connections in the relevant offices. The Province's Irrigation Department sent investigators who conducted their own survey and confirmed that the river's water volume was sufficient for two canals. Soon, the necessary permits were issued. When the Grand Harmony Canal was completed in 1934, the county magistrate of Anyang personally visited the site and oversaw the redistribution of water flows between the old and new irrigation communities. Out of the ten gates that directed water from the Anyang River, the old canal community received seven, while the new canal was allocated three.

By that time, Zhang was already in the US. He was too far away and likely too busy to monitor the progress of the canal project he had helped to initiate. When he returned in the spring of 1935, he discovered that new complications had arisen with the Grand Harmony Canal. Shortly after settling in Nanjing for his first job back in China, he received a letter from his father informing him that resentment over sharing water had led the neighboring irrigation community to sabotage the canal, causing substantial damage. The opposing community consisted of several villages and had better connections to local authorities. They had previously obstructed the canal's construction and had now forcefully blocked part of it, rendering it inoperative. It was clear that the people of Xiahan, including his father, had been waiting for Zhang's return to resolve the situation. Since the Grand Harmony Canal had been fully authorized by the local and provincial governments, Zhang decided to address the issue through official channels. He brought the case directly to Chiang Kai-shek's office. The response was swift: with the backing of the highest office in the land, local officials quickly intervened to end the sabotage and punish the perpetrators.

The next major "favor" Zhang did for the people in Anyang involved a much larger area. In July 1946, after Japan's surrender the previous year, Zhang made his first home visit since the war began in 1937. However, CCP forces, having gained strength through their guerrilla warfare during the conflict, had launched radical land reforms in the territories under their control to win the support of the poor and prepare for a final showdown with the KMT. The epic class war in China was about to begin. In Anyang, the Communists controlled two-thirds of the county's rural areas, where landlords and wealthy peasants were deprived of their land and, in many cases, beaten to death due to the violence associated with these land reforms. Thousands fled their homes and sought refuge in the county seat. Xiahan village had also fallen to the Communists, so Zhang was unable to visit his family home, despite being back on Anyang soil.

Refugees from many fallen villages gathered in the county seat to celebrate Zhang's return, asking for his help in fighting back and reclaiming their lost homes and land. They organized into a militia, a common formation during the CCP land reforms, called the "Home-Reclaiming Regiment (*huanxiang tuan*)." While the militia had a sufficient number of fighters, they lacked enough weapons and ammunition. Zhang leveraged his newly acquired status as a member of the National Political Consultation Assembly and tapped into his connections with the military stationed in Anyang, which was tasked with the defense of the city rather than the reclamation of lost villages in the countryside. Eventually, he secured over 1,000 rifles and 50,000 rounds of ammunition for the regiment. One of his earliest teachers from his homeschooling days was elected as the commander. After some training, and with assistance from the regular military, the militia was able to reclaim more than 30 villages the following year.

It is evident that Zhang was devoted to his home place and eager to engage in its local affairs. However, despite the apparent scenario of a successful local son helping his community, it is difficult to argue that he was merely providing aid to those in need. In fact, the need was mutual. The recognition and respect of the people in his home community were as important as—if not more essential than—his accomplishments in the outside world. Anyang was not only the initial stage where Zhang's life evolved, but it also represented his intended final destination when his journey in the world came to a close. Traditional literati often used the metaphor of a tree's roots and leaves to describe a man's life: as a tree grows taller, its branches spread wide, and its leaves multiply, but ultimately, when the leaves fall, they return to where the roots are. For Zhang, his home place was where his roots lay. What could be more important than that?

In terms of being a native son rooted in his home place, poised to return, and ready to serve, Zhang was no different from Cui, Ma, and hundreds of thousands of other literati from earlier times and other places. Regarding a gentleman's bond to his local community, a Ming dynasty scholar once remarked that "there is no escaping what the folks of the home community expect and entrust to you; you fulfill it, if not in the morning, then in the evening, if not by consoling them, then by providing for them."[12] This age-old attachment to the home place, which has been an integral part of the literati mentality, was, it is fair to say, inherited by modern intellectuals.

There are, of course, differences in the bond to one's native place between Zhang and his late imperial counterparts. While the polity-locality relationship still retains an aggregate structure, it is now infused with the new concept of "local self-governance." For instance, a county was no longer administered solely by a court-appointed magistrate and a handful of his associates. Instead, elected officials—often emerging from voluntary associations within the local community—became officially involved in governance. The weak central state during the Republican era, even following the KMT unification, meant that this legitimate exercise of influence by local elites was not merely theoretical but often a reality. In 1932, for example, when a corrupt magistrate who had embezzled a substantial amount of tax money was about to be reassigned somewhere else, several local leaders mobilized the public, stormed the county government, arrested the magistrate, and paraded him through the streets. All four organizers of this incident were also involved in the county gazetteer project. The magistrate was eventually convicted in court, while the same court released the organizers, who had been detained by higher authorities shortly after the incident. The channel through which these local elites sought justice, that is, directly arresting a corrupt official and parading him through streets, did not follow the official procedure. But the boldness of their action reflects exactly the sense of agency among the local elites that was not seen during the imperial era. The enthusiasm of the local society for compiling and publishing their own county gazetteer can largely be attributed to this newly gained sense of agency.

As a professor of political science, Zhang wrote several books specifically addressing the issue of central-local relations. His stated goal in these works was to elaborate on and illuminate Sun Yat-sen's theory of local self-governance, which he referred to as "the doctrine of power-balance." As the name suggests, this doctrine aims to maintain a balance between the powers retained by the central government and those granted to local entities. However, it differs from Montesquieu's concept of "checks and balances." As Zhang explains, this doctrine views the power relationship between the central and local governments not as a zero-sum game, but as cohesive. Both levels of government share a common goal: the effective governance of the nation. Therefore, the division of power follows the principle of maximum efficiency, where functions that can be conveniently managed by the central government are assigned to it, while those that can be effectively handled by local authorities remain with them. In practical terms, governmental functions concerning the nation as a whole, such as diplomacy and defense, should be controlled by the central government. Conversely, functions more relevant to local governance, such as policing, should be managed by local governments. As a result, local authorities gain a significant voice on issues that directly affect their well-being, allowing them to take greater initiative.[13]

Related to the concept and practice of "local self-governance" is another significant shift in the native-place bond of modern intellectuals. As "local self-governance" became institutionalized, the influence of local elites transitioned from informal to formal. In the past, the influence of individuals like Cui and Ma in Anyang was primarily based on their reputation and status. While much of Zhang's influence also stemmed from his connections and experiences, the emergence of offices representing the local community—specifically charged with voicing their interests and concerns—inevitably redirected people's attention and energy toward these new venues and channels. Over time, local elections would become the new focus of political activity in the community, bringing about different dynamics in local life. For example, in the old days an educated individual could only hold office and gain power elsewhere and reap recognition back home in the native place, but now he (and increasingly, even she) could hold office and gain power in the home locale. What he need from the local folks would be not only praises and respect, but also their votes.

The new political landscape arrived quite suddenly. Sun Yat-sen envisioned that after the military unification, the country would enter a brief period of "tutelary rule," during which the KMT would train the populace in self-governance before transitioning to formal constitutional rule. This period was originally planned to last six years, but Chiang Kai-shek postponed it with various excuses. By the end of the prolonged war with Japan, however, there were few reasonable justifications for delaying the end of tutelary rule. In 1946, despite the heightened military tensions between the CCP and the KMT, Chiang decided to initiate constitutional governance. A constitutional assembly was called. It passed the constitution at the end of that year, and elections for the legislative body—corresponding roughly to the House of Representatives in the US Congress—were scheduled to begin in 1947. Once the new legislative body was established, the semi-constitutional National Political Consultation Assembly would be dissolved.

As a member of the Consultation Assembly, Zhang was expected to run for a seat in the new legislature. At his prime age, with a flourishing career and high hopes for the country's future, Zhang was more than happy to meet these expectations. It was soon decided that he would run for a seat representing the second legislative district of Henan, a district centered on Anyang County that roughly corresponded to the old Zhangde Prefecture. In fact, Zhang's trip to Anyang in July 1946 was partly aimed at gauging the local political climate and reconnecting with the community in preparation for a potential election campaign. As a political science professor, Zhang had clearly anticipated the advent of constitutional rule and the inevitable changes it would bring to the political landscape.

The trip went exceptionally well. Liu Leshan, the head of Anyang's local security militia, along with Huang Boying, the head of the local KMT Youth League, and the Anyang branch director of the Peasant Bank—one of the four major nationwide banks—traveled nearly a hundred miles from the county seat to welcome him. They formed sworn brotherhoods and pledged to help one another. Upon returning to the county seat, Zhang established another sworn brotherhood with a group of local grandees, including Wang Zhiquan, who had been one of the most notorious bandit leaders in the area over the past decades. Wang had since been co-opted into the KMT military system and held the rank of general. He soon introduced Zhang to his own sworn brother Guo Qing, another former bandit who was now a leader of the security force in Anyang. Together, they registered a new industrial company named "New Hope" as the organizational basis for their "common enterprise."

The election procedure required that candidates be nominated by political parties. The CCP, believing that real power comes only from the barrel of a gun, chose not to participate. As a result, the KMT became the only major party in the election. Utilizing his connections in the province, Zhang easily secured his candidacy by the fall of 1947. The second district of Henan was entitled to send 6 legislators to the national legislature; the KMT Henan branch nominated 11 candidates. The campaign season officially began in 1948, amid a fully developed civil war. Zhang returned to Anyang in February via military airplane to campaign on the ground.

In some respects, the election culture and the way Zhang ran his campaign might appear unusual to those accustomed to modern election campaigns in the US. The leaders of the county's militia could influence local officials—both elected and appointed—who, in turn, greatly affected how people in their jurisdiction voted. Inviting individuals for paid meals was an effective strategy for swaying their votes. However, on a deeper level, many of the mechanisms and strategies employed—such as securing the support of powerful and influential figures, garnering substantial votes through their backing, and hosting special events to court public favor—are not so different from practices in modern democracies. In this regard, Zhang was in a privileged position. He was the beloved son of Anyang, the largest county in the district. The heads of the county's ten districts were significantly influenced by the militia chief Liu Lexian, who was his sworn brother. Additionally, the chief minister of the region constituting the legislative district, Zhao Zhichen, was a former middle school teacher of Zhang's, as was Zhang Tianji, the chair of the Anyang County council. Although as a professor Zhang was not wealthy, the former bandit leader Wang Zhiquan provided him with funds to host influential individuals for dinners, fostering connections. In some instances, resembling a more established democracy, Zhang delivered public speeches to people in the market, to soldiers in the local security force's garrison, and to members of various civil associations in their headquarters.

Zhang's campaign was a success. In April, he was back in Nanjing. A telegram from Wang Zhiquan informed him that he had received 260,000 votes, ranking first among the six elected. The first session of the Republic of China's legislative body opened in May 1948. However, by that time, the country was entering its third year of civil war. The CCP had endured the hardships of the war's initial stages, and the tide was turning against the KMT. In just a few months, three final military campaigns would commence, effectively destroying Chiang Kai-shek's military forces on the mainland and paving the way for the founding of the People's Republic of China in October 1949. The rapid change in the situation was undoubtedly a disaster for Chiang and the KMT, and in some respects, they deserved it due to the party's rampant corruption and profound ineffectiveness. They would later regret their actions and seek reform after retreating to Taiwan. The election of 1948, and the democracy it represented, marked the final triumph of the ideas of "local self-governance." Yet, it also signaled the last swan song for such ideals in the Republic of China (Figure 8).

However, it would be misguided to dismiss the election of 1948 and Zhang's campaign efforts as merely an insignificant detour in history. For one thing, the Communist takeover in China was far from inevitable. A complex set of geopolitical and military contingencies, both international and domestic, converged to propel the CCP to power. Without Communist disruption, local self-governance and democracy were likely to progress on the Chinese mainland. In fact, even in the face of Communist disruption, the election was undeniably legitimate and achieved its intended objectives. Moreover, both the institutional frameworks of democracy and the ideals of local self-governance were carried by the KMT to Taiwan, where they eventually flourished after navigating a series of challenges. Zhang, for his part, would go on to serve as a legislator for decades in the Republic of China in Taiwan.

In light of this, when we consider the longer history of the human-place relationship in China, the election of 1948, Zhang's campaign, and his overall involvement in the local affairs of Anyang can be seen as early efforts to transform the millennium-old tradition of literati localism and adapt it to the local politics of a modern republic. Times had changed. So had the institutional settings and the political and social environments. Both the localities and the locally rooted people needed to evolve

Figure 8 Voting scene in 1948, Shanghai. (Source: *Wikipedia*, "1948年立法委员选举.")

accordingly. Both came close to succeeding: the former experienced an unprecedented surge of vitality, while the latter experimented with new ways of engaging with their home places. However, the military debacle of the KMT shocked everyone and dramatically altered the landscape. With the Communist takeover, everything was reset.

4
The death of hometown

The strength of the Communist Party came from its discipline and willingness to sacrifice its individual members. Regarding these qualities, Joseph Stalin once proclaimed that the Communists were "people of a special mold […] made of a special stuff." The early Communists in China, whose conversions were often made at great personal risk, provided abundant examples of this specificity. One of the earliest converts recruited by Mao in Hunan was Xia Minghan, whose famous poem that he recited at the moment of his execution in 1928 states, "My head being chopped off bears no importance, as long as the 'ism' I am after is the truth." Xia's younger brother also died as a Communist martyr in the same year. His sister-in-law, Zeng Zhi, another early Communist convert in Hunan, remarried, to a CCP comrade. In 1932, the couple agreed to sell their baby boy to fund the operations of the party branch in Amoy.

The founder of the first CCP branch in Anyang, He Shu, also hailed from Hunan. He Shu and his wife, Zhu Shunhua, were both early converts personally recruited to the party by Mao. In fact, it was Mao and his first wife who introduced He and Zhu to each other. In the summer of 1922, only a few months after the CCP's founding, He Shu was sent to Anyang to guide the labor movement due to the relatively large number of industrial workers at the Anyang Railway Station. He successfully recruited three new members to the CCP, shared basic knowledge about the Communist Party, formed a branch, and was soon reassigned to tasks elsewhere. In 1929, He Shu and his wife were arrested in Hunan. During their interrogation, the interrogators tortured them by disemboweling their two-year-old son in front of their eyes. Ultimately, all five of their children were killed by the KMT. Despite these horrific experiences, the couple remained CCP members throughout their lives.

Such steel-like discipline among the Communists, along with their willingness to make the ultimate sacrifice, was built upon what is known as "proletariat consciousness," or the Communist sense of historical agency. In the words of Georg Lukács, it is through proletariat consciousness that the Communist overcomes the limitations of nearsightedness and immediate interests, seeing society "from the center, as a coherent whole." Vladimir Lenin's classic elaboration elevates proletariat consciousness to the status of omniscience:

> Working-class consciousness cannot be genuine political consciousness unless the workers are trained to respond to *all* cases of tyranny, oppression, violence, and abuse, *no matter what class* is affected [...]. The consciousness of the working masses cannot be genuine class-consciousness, unless the workers learn, from concrete, and above all from topical, political facts and events to observe *every other* social class in *all* the manifestations of its intellectual, ethical, and political life

> [...]. The self-knowledge of the working class is indissolubly bound up, not solely with a fully clear theoretical understanding—or rather, not so much with the theoretical, as with the practical, understanding—of the relationships between *all* the various classes of modern society, acquired through the experience of political life. (emphasis original)[14]

From the ability to see through everything, there comes what Lukács called the ability to "go beyond the contingencies of history" and to "act in such a way to change reality." In the words of Lenin, the proletariat consciousness entails the "coincidence of theory and practice" whereby the Communist can "consciously throw the weight of its action onto the scales of history." What these theoretically dense statements mean in simpler terms is that proletariat consciousness endows the Communist with a conviction that he or she is in possession of the absolute truth, a conviction that leads them to act as the agent of the inevitable historical progress, with the ultimate sense of invincibility. It was this conviction that came with the proletariat consciousness, or rather this conviction that constitutes the proletariat consciousness, that made it possible for the Communists to bear the unbearable and deny conventional human feelings. This is, to some degree, not unlike religious feelings whereby the people can find the meaning of both their own lives and the cause they are devoted to.

Fascination with the power of proletariat consciousness to transform people's thoughts, behaviors, and personalities was common among the founding generation of the CCP. This may be attributed to the unique characteristics of the intellectuals who came of age during the New Culture Movement. They arrived on the historical stage with no fixed social status or moral convictions yet embraced the daunting task of both saving the nation and transforming society. Once the most radical among them committed to Marxism-Leninism as the solution to all problems, they naturally focused on its central theory of historical agency, particularly the concept of proletariat consciousness.

Efforts to instill and enhance proletariat consciousness among party members spanned the entire history of the CCP, continuing up until its takeover of power in 1949—and even beyond. Part of Mao's motivation in launching the Great Proletarian Cultural Revolution was to retain the spirit of the proletariat when he perceived it declining among his comrades. However, adhering strictly to the logic of proletariat consciousness also transformed Communist members into instruments of the proletariat cause, making it difficult for them to affiliate with any particularistic interests. In fact, the strengthening of discipline and the sacrificial spirit within the party went hand in hand with the suppression of these particularistic affiliations.

Historiography has identified two significant waves of thought transformation within the CCP. The first was the "Bolshevization" of the young party, which occurred between the CCP's founding in 1921 and the disastrous end of its United Front with the KMT in 1927. This process involved intellectual converts to Marxism-Leninism transitioning "from friend to comrade." The completion of this transformation has been variously marked as occurring at the Emergency Conference of August 7, 1927, when absolute obedience to the party's resolutions became mandatory for CCP members, or at the CCP's Sixth Congress in 1928, when the absolute correctness of the party line—presumably reflecting proletariat consciousness—was firmly established.[15] By either chronology, the paramount importance of the party was firmly established by its conclusion. The second significant wave is the Rectification Movement, officially launched between 1942 and 1944, which recurred periodically until the end of the Mao era. The Rectification Movement is often recognized as the Sinicization of Marxism-Leninism, leading to the rise of Maoism, which helped the CCP build consensus and discipline.

A consistent theme that runs through both the "Bolshevization" of the 1920s and the "Rectification" of the 1940s is the transformation of the CCP from any particularistic affiliations toward a party grounded in a commitment to a common ideology—whether it be Marxism-Leninism or Maoism. In other words, there was a continuous process of what the CCP refers to as "party-building" (*dangjian*), one crucial goal of which is to forge a "party spirit" (*dangxing*) among its cadres. This spirit ensures that proletariat consciousness prevails over any selfish concerns, while a universalistic orientation eliminates all particularistic attachments.

In between these two waves, the emphasis on cultivating proletariat consciousness and attacking particularistic attachments—championed by Mao and other party leaders—never wavered. Mao's famous essay "Against Liberalism," written in Yan'an in September 1937, identified fellow native-place men along with classmates, colleagues, and other familiar social relations as areas of special concern where "petit bourgeoisie" selfishness—the primary obstacle to proletariat consciousness—might emerge. The most influential document on CCP party-building prior to the Rectification Movement was Liu Shaoqi's *How to Be a Good*

Communist. Liu, a Moscow-trained theorist and the would-be inventor of the term "Mao Thought," elaborated on the concept of proletariat consciousness using clear Marxist-Leninist language in this classic work:

> A Communist should think about and prioritize the *general* interest of the party on every issue and at every time [...]. To sacrifice one's interest or even one's life for the party, the class, the national liberation, and the liberation of humanity, with no hesitation, even with joy: this is the highest Communist morality, the highest principle for a party member; this is the pure and powerful demonstration of the proletariat consciousness.
>
> ...
>
> A Communist party member is no longer ordinary people but rather awakened proletariat vanguard; he should not represent his personal interest, but rather the representative of the awakened class interest and class consciousness; he is already the representative of the *generalized* class. (emphasis added)[16]

The consistency with Lenin is readily apparent here, as Liu also invoked proletariat consciousness to elevate the Communists beyond all personal limitations in perspective and interest, transforming them into a non-personal instrument of universal historical progress. The momentum for thought reform continued unabated. In July 1941, on the twentieth anniversary of the party's founding, Mao personally drafted the CCP resolution to "enhance party spirit." This resolution emphasized the importance of "unity, centralization, and obedience to the center" of the party and identified "individualism," "heroism," and "independence" as primary targets of criticism.

When all the intellectual and organizational preparations were complete and the social and political conditions were ripe, the Rectification Movement was finally launched in 1942. Through this movement, Mao successfully established his supreme dominance in both the theoretical and political spheres of the party. While the attacks on doctrinism—associated with Mao's inner-party challengers who were better connected with Moscow—were crucial to the movement, the overall goal of the Rectification remained consistent with the ongoing thought reform: the unity, discipline, and centralization of the party. However, the center of authority was now Mao, rather than Moscow.

In one of the key documents of the Rectification Movement, "Rectify the Party's Style of Work," Mao unequivocally articulated the principle of Democratic Centralism, first defined by Lenin: "Every party member, and every work in the party, every speech and action, must take the perspective of the party as a whole." The immediate target of this document was factionalism within the party. Nonetheless, it is clear that for the party at this time, the relationship between the part and the whole was substantially different from that of the late imperial literati or Mao's own youth; the whole was no longer merely an aggregation of the parts but consumed them.

The understanding of the part-whole relationship among CCP members that became the norm after the Rectification Movement can be illustrated by a collection of theoretical articles titled *Human Nature, Party Spirit, and Individuality*, written by leading party propaganda officials. One of the articles, authored by Chen Boda, Mao's deputy on ideological issues, stated that "being a Communist Party member means removing all partial and limited interests and obeying the interests of the class as a whole." Another article asserted that a Communist Party member must "consider the party's interests as a whole and ensure that individual interests align with, and eventually dissolve into, that whole." In a different context, Deng Liqun, who later became the chief of the CCP's Central Propaganda Department, argued that a proletariat viewpoint is "exactly the viewpoint of the whole."

Such a mentality necessitates universalism in human-place relationships. After the CCP took power in China, the Communists, seeking to remake the country in their own image, went great lengths to suppress, if not completely erase, local sentiments from the political culture of the People's Republic. For example, a governor of Shandong Province was purged after reportedly stating, "I am a native of Shandong; I am for the people of Shandong and the cadres of Shandong."[17] Such local sentiment is incompatible with the universalistic orientation embodied in the Communist persona, most vividly summarized by Mao in 1944:

> We hail from all corners (of the realm) and have joined together for a common revolutionary objective. […] Our cadres must show concern for every soldier, and all people in the revolutionary ranks must care for each other, must love and help each other.[18]

Parallel to the discipline imposed on Communist cadres was the taming of locality. The land reform effectively dissolved—and often physically destroyed—the gentry class in the countryside, while similar reforms targeted old elites in the cities, modern professionals, and contemporary institutions. With the social elites gone, society was leveled, becoming what the philosopher Hannah Arendt referred to as a "classless society."

As party branches penetrating every rural village and urban block, the new party-state achieved total control. Local places still existed, but they become mere administrative entities, losing their significance as home places for the local elites. As a result, local places lost their characters, and became consumed by the national whole. Concrete illustrations of this mechanism abound: the Tiananmen Tower and the socialist motherland replaced the native soil and local custom as the beginning point of history and geography education for schoolchildren; shrines to local worthies were replaced by cemeteries of revolutionary martyrs who were rarely local natives, and soon even the very term "local worthies 鄉賢" was forgotten; the compilation of local gazetteers ceased and, when it resumed decades later, became a mere function of local bureaucracies, stripped of its former charm.

There were still discussions about granting localities more leeway and allowing them greater initiative, as Mao himself famously advocated in 1956.[19] However, there is a significant difference between this "centralized decentralization" ordained from the center and "decentralization as a pre-nationalist 'fact of nature,'" as described by the American Sinologist Joseph Levenson. Mao's approach embodied the confidence of a conqueror who had completely subdued the locality and rendered it docile. Levenson used a metaphor to illustrate the fate of localities (in his case, at the provincial level) in Communist China: what the Maoist state did to its local components was akin to "killing the blooms (or certifying the deaths) of provincial selves" and then, rather than discarding them, pressing them into a national album. In this process, localities were transformed "from divisive single spectacles to which the provinces gave themselves" into "a diversified repertoire to which the nation gave attention." In this sense, the classless society of Mao's China was also "local-less."

The best illustration of the "local-less" society in Mao's China is perhaps Mao's own experience of revisiting his home village, Shaoshan, where he had deep family roots and where he conducted some of his earliest Communist activities. In 1959, Mao finally returned to his home village that he had left behind 32 years before. The moment of the eventual homecoming must have been soothing and relaxed, as indicated by the smiles in one of the most famous photos from the Mao era and in the poem "Shaoshan Revisited" that Mao wrote for the reunion:

> Like a dim dream recalled, I curse the long-fled
>   past—
> My native soil two and thirty years gone by.
> The red flag roused the serf, halberd in hand,
> While the despot's black talons held his whip aloft.
> Bitter sacrifice strengthens bold resolve,
> Which dares to make sun and moon shine in new
>   skies.
> Happy, I see wave upon wave of paddy and beans,
> And all around, heroes home-bound in the
>   evening mist.

The soft feelings associated with the passage of time and the memories of one's ancestral home are as human as those expressed by anyone at any time. However, the veteran Communist revolutionary, who was then vying to be the leader of the proletarian revolution worldwide, conceptualized his home locality not merely as a place of nostalgia but as a site of class warfare, where the melancholy of homesickness transformed into the beauty of resolve, sacrifice, struggle, and the triumph of the awakened masses. The key to this poetic imagination—just as it was the key to the revolution's success—was proletariat consciousness. This consciousness dramatized the people of the home locale as class antagonists while generalizing strangers elsewhere as class brothers. The famous photo in which Mao stands amid young pioneers, wearing a red scarf himself, perfectly conveys the ethos of a leader beloved by *the* people. However, it reveals little about *a* native son's homecoming to *a* place where he was once rooted and his reception by the local community (Figure 9).

Ideally, as the founders of the CCP made clear, true Communists should also avoid national patriotism, as the class interests of the proletariat form an indivisible whole, and their struggle against the capitalist class takes place on a global stage, transcending national boundaries. However, the Chinese Communists' aspiration to transcend nationalism often fell short. Part of this can be attributed to the origins of Communism in China: it emerged as a solution to the nation's problem of salvation. Chinese Communists embraced Marxism-Leninism not solely for its theoretical appeal but for its political effectiveness; its utopian vision provided desperate seekers with a clear common goal, while its party-building methods served as a "unifying principle of concerted action." As Communists, they could not easily forget their national mission. In a certain sense, Communism was fulfilling a role in China that, strictly speaking, belonged to nationalism—that of establishing an effective state for their own nation.

Figure 9 Mao back to Shaoshan Village, 1959. (Source: 凤凰网[20])

The Nationalist Party (KMT), of course, sought to achieve similar goals. Sun Yat-sen's original vision for a Chinese republic bore clear influences from American democracy, although he was also wary of the dangerous gap between the rich and the poor that unrestrained capitalism could create. After his initial project was derailed by ambitious politicians and entrenched warlords, Sun became increasingly attracted to the Soviet Union, primarily for its proven techniques in building a centralized and effective political party. His concern for equality certainly made him more sympathetic to socialist ideas, but he remained unwilling to accept the doctrine of class warfare. The Soviet Union was willing to help Sun nonetheless, and as far as Sun was willing to go, the Chinese Communists followed him and injected the KMT with tremendous organizational and propaganda energies during the several years the two parties worked together for the Northern Expedition. But not everyone in the KMT was willing to tolerate the radical social programs of the Communists. Chiang Kai-shek, for example, held a strong aversion to these initiatives and sought to purge the Communists as soon as he had the opportunity.

Chiang, like most conservative nationalists, hoped that after unification, affairs in China could be conducted in the usual way. Particularistic ties were part of the "old way" that he wished to preserve. Throughout his life, Chiang maintained a strong attachment to his home locale and particularly trusted his fellow natives. The kind of favors and protections that Zhang Jinjian received from Chen Guofu throughout his career—practices that became targets of party discipline and thought reform under the CCP—were considered perfectly normal within the KMT, as they were acceptable in varying degrees elsewhere.

However, China was not a "usual" country, and the first half of the twentieth century was no usual time. Long-term poverty, acute economic distress, and the entrenched abuse of power at every level of society had left people desperate and the social fabric fragile. Warlordism and imperialism, which were high-profile targets of the Nationalist Revolution, represented only surface-level issues and were perhaps not the most difficult to address. At a deeper, grassroots level, basic decency faced tremendous challenges, and daily life had long been brutalized.

The unusual methods that Zheng Zhi employed to fund the party, along with the extremely inhumane torture suffered by He Shu and his wife, were not accidents or anomalies. Selling one's wife and children to survive crises had been effectively legalized since the early nineteenth century under the Qing dynasty. Burying people alive was a common form of punishment in rural North China throughout modern times. During the warlord era, some bandits in Anyang, for instance, claimed the harvest of a peasant's farm. After discovering that the peasant had secretly harvested some of the crops, they forced him to bury his young son alive. Wang Zhiquan, a bandit leader who survived the Japanese occupation, faced a choice between the CCP and the KMT at the end of the war. To make an unequivocal proclamation of his decision, he buried his boyhood friend alive because that friend was sent by the CCP to win him over. In such a brutalized society, the usual methods that Chiang Kai-shek and other conservatives preferred were ineffective for mobilizing the vast majority of the population.

The CCP's social programs and political agendas, being framed by the idea of class warfare, would inevitably cause more hatred and violence in an already brutalized society of modern China. They could even hold special attractions because of this. If the CCP's success required the sacrifice of conventional human feelings, the Communists were willing to pay that price. Extreme atrocities during the land reforms were rampant. Oral and documented accounts from Anyang present apocalyptic imagery: internal organs hanging from tree branches, horses dragging people—heads hanging down to the ground—across fields dotted with post-harvest corn stalks, among other horrors.

The resoluteness to fight generated by such "class antagonism" certainly positioned the Communists favorably during the civil war. Combined with the religious-like devotion of its cadres as well as the strategic and tactic geniuses of its leaders, the CCP was able to achieve what had eluded the Nationalist Party for two generations and to build a powerful state unprecedented in history. However, in this process, all types of particularistic ties were sacrificed. Ultimately, one could say that the collapse of the balance between locality and polity, along with the suppression of local sentiment, were among the costs the new nation-state paid for its ride with Communism.

The toll that Communism took on local sentiments and other conventional human feelings, as well as the unusual commitment it inspired, is evident in the experiences of Zhang's peers in Anyang who joined the CCP. Guo Shengyong left home for Guangzhou with Xu Xiangqian in the summer of 1925, shortly after graduating from middle school, along with more than 20 fellow students. His wife and their two-year-old daughter accompanied him to the edge of the village. She made two pairs of shoes—one for her husband and the other for Xu. Guo told his wife to wait for him. She waited for him for the rest of her life, though Guo's life was cut short in 1929 when he was executed by the KMT. Another alumnus of the middle school, Ma Zai, survived all the terrors and wars, eventually living to an old age as a Communist.

Ma Zai (1905–1992) was born and raised in a village just a few miles west of Zhang's Xiahan. He was the youngest son of a well-to-do peasant family. In 1924, he graduated from middle school, a year ahead of Zhang and Guo. Troubled by the social conditions in Anyang at the time, particularly after his father was kidnapped twice by bandits, Ma became convinced that the only way to save the country and transform society was for educated men to take up arms.

In the spring of 1925, without telling anyone, he left home and joined the student army in the provincial capital. This student army was a new type of military force being experimented with by a provincial warlord who also believed in arming educated men. Through letters from friends who had not yet graduated from middle school in Anyang, Ma learned about Xu and the Huangpu Military Academy. Therefore, when the academy opened a recruitment office in Henan, he applied. By the end of the year, Ma had arrived in Guangzhou and enrolled as a cadet in the military academy, alongside Guo and his other middle school friends.

At the academy, Ma witnessed the growing tension between the two political parties. He felt an affinity for the Communists and joined the CCP in October 1926, shortly after the Northern Expedition began. Ma's decision was not surprising, given his disdain for the common life philosophy embodied by Chiang Kai-shek—a philosophy that many of his fellow cadets at the academy and colleagues in the Nationalist Revolution admired. In Ma's own words, it was a philosophy that sought "glamor, wealth, and elevated status," something Ma believed a true revolutionary should rise above.

In the summer of 1927, Ma was appointed political commissar of a military unit and marched to Wuhan. It is a coincidence of fate that, during the three nights when Zhang and Guo discussed the country's political situation and Zhang's career choice, Ma was in the same city, along with several other alumni of Anyang Middle School who had attended the military academy. However, they would soon part ways and never see each other again for the rest of their lives.

When Communists became targets of state persecution during the civil war, Ma was sent back to Anyang by the party to organize peasant and labor movements. He soon became the head of the CCP's Anyang branch. To fund the party's activities, the group once decided to steal cotton from a field at night and sell it. When it came time to choose which farm to steal from, Ma volunteered his own family farm. To organize miners in the nearby Liuhegou coal mine, he took a job as a miner himself, enduring the full extent of the harsh conditions alongside the working men digging coal in the darkness. This made him appear as a "weirdo" in the eyes of his family and neighbors, who saw an educated and promising young man returning home as a social wreck. However, he was soon accepted by the miners as one of their own. A successful strike in 1932 forced the mine's management to raise wages, which also helped increase CCP membership among the miners.

In the winter of 1930, Liu Shaoqi, an experienced labor organizer for the party, visited the Liuhegou mine. A photo was taken of Liu, Ma, and other CCP comrades after they successfully survived a police hunt through close cooperation. Although the photo was meant to commemorate their success and should have featured the men in formal attire, the tied bottoms of their trouser legs—a common style of the poor in northern China—made it clear that working in the mine had made Ma almost indistinguishable from the miners in appearance (Figure 10).

In the last months of 1932, the CCP branches in several counties of northern Henan plotted a revolt. When the revolt failed, Ma and other leaders were arrested and imprisoned in Beijing. In 1937, after the outbreak of the total war with Japan, they broke out of prison. From that point on, Ma's career never intersected with Anyang again. He became a leader of one of the Communist "base areas" behind enemy lines during the War of Resistance and participated in the development of the famous "tunnel warfare" in the North China Plain. During the renewed civil war between

Figure 10 Photo of Ma Zai (left) and Liu Shaoqi (second from left) together with other Communists working at Liuhegou Mine. 1930. (Source: Liuheguo Museum)

the KMT and the CCP, Ma led the land reform in one of the northern provinces. After the founding of the PRC, he worked in several industries at the party's direction, covering a wide geographic range from the southern province of Hunan to the northwestern province of Xinjiang, though he mostly remained in Beijing. Ma visited Anyang after his retirement, where he was received by the local party committee, of which he had been one of the earliest leaders. Before his death, he wrote a memoir titled *My Life of Battles*, in which he referred to his wife, another Communist who died in battle, as his closest comrade. However, little was said about his personal life, family, or ancestral homeland. What Ma did not mention at all in his memoir was his first wife, a woman named Liu Chunlan, whom he left behind in his home village in Anyang, along with the son and daughter Liu bore him. Like Guo, Ma married early in life. And like Guo, his family suffered greatly due to his revolutionary activities. For both Guo and Ma, family and hometown ties were among the sacrifices made for a universal cause.

However, this did not mean they were numb to the usual familial and local sentiments. During their academy days, their fellow Anyang natives often gathered together on weekends, wrestling, discussing politics, and sharing information. Ma noted in his memoir that those were his most joyful days. After the Communist takeover, Ma wrote home, attempting to reconnect with his family and ensure that his son and daughter were on the right career paths. Eventually, his daughter by Liu Chunlan left Anyang to join him at his new post in the PRC. As a Communist, Ma was expected to suppress these personal feelings, and he certainly tried, as did Guo and hundreds of thousands of other

Communists. When they couldn't entirely suppress these particularistic connections, they made sure not to speak of them. It was through these self-imposed collective disciplinary efforts that locality and local sentiment, once integral to traditional Chinese civilization, nearly vanished from the lives of political elites under Mao.

In contrast, Zhang Jinjian, the conservative, was a model family man and local patriot. The urge to take family members and relatives under his wing was almost natural. His younger brother, Jinxi, who joined him in destroying the village temple in 1928, shadowed him during some of his postings before his departure for the US in 1931. Through Zhang's guidance (and perhaps also because of his connections), Jinxi was enrolled in the military academy and pursued a military career during the war. When the KMT lost the civil war, Jinxi retreated to Taiwan with the government.

Another brother, Jinsheng, who was nine years younger, served as a telecommunication officer in the military. During the final stages of the civil war, Jinsheng was stationed in Beijing. Zhang's father, seeing the inevitable loss of northern China to the Communists, cited family emergencies repeatedly to urge him to quit his job and come to Nanjing. Jinsheng complied. Zhang found a position for his youngest brother in Taiwan before the final collapse of the KMT. When Jinsheng reported to his new post in Taiwan, he brought their parents with him. By the time Zhang Jinjian and his family moved to Taiwan, all the Zhangs—father and sons and grandchildren—were resettled there.

Zhang had two younger sisters. One was 19 years younger than he and died soon after marriage. The other, Jinlan, was 12 years younger. When Zhang revisited Anyang in 1946, the village of Jinlan and her husband had fallen under Communist control, just like their native village Xiahan. Zhang managed to get Jinlan, her husband, and their two daughters out of the Communist area and brought them all to Nanjing. In addition to taking care of his own family during this trip back to Anyang, Zhang also managed to find the widow and daughter of his middle school friend, Guo Shengyong. It had been more than 20 years since Guo left home with the Communist teacher Xu Xiangqian. His wife, not knowing anything about his life or death since then, was still waiting for him. His daughter, now in her mid-twenties, had married. Zhang gave the wife some money and helped find better jobs for the daughter and her husband.

After leaving Anyang, Jinjian found a position for Jinlan's husband in the KMT military. During an operation in the northwestern province of Shaanxi, Jinlan's husband did not return. Eventually, Jinlan and her two daughters joined her natal family and resettled in Taiwan. With that, Zhang had all of his parents, siblings, and their children moved from Anyang to Taiwan. There was another member of this extended family: a daughter of his cousin Jinbang. Jinbang was Zhang's uncle's son, 19 years younger than Jinjian. When the home village fell to the Communists, Jinbang was able to escape with his own family. Zhang found a job for Jinbang in the KMT-controlled area and brought one of his daughters to Taiwan. Because of Zhang's significant contributions to the well-being of this extended family, his two younger brothers insisted on performing the ritual of bowing to him on New Year's

Day after their father's death. Zhang had, perhaps accidentally, become the new patriarch of a transplanted Anyang patriarchal family in Taiwan. He was reluctant to accept the ritual bowing from his younger brothers, but on the other hand, Zhang was quite committed to continuing the Anyang local rituals when it was his turn to perform them for others. During his mother's funeral in 1964, for example, the 62-year-old Zhang kowtowed to all the guests according to the Anyang custom.

Aside from Zhang's own attachment to his native place, the fact that the Anyang customs were observed in Taiwan was also made possible by another factor: there was a Anyang sojourner community of considerable size on the island. The origin of that community may serve as the most dramatic demonstration of how the modern counterparts of the literati utilized their connections in the wider world to support their home locale.

The story of how this community originated dates back to the summer of 1946, when Zhang returned to Anyang to prepare for his election campaign the following year. The Communist guerrillas' sabotage of the railroad had turned the county seat of Anyang into an isolated city filled with thousands of refugees from the countryside, students in the middle schools, and huge piles of cotton, the proudest local cash crop typically shipped out by railway. Cotton merchants, stranded in the county seat, were quickly running out of cash and desperately needed to sell their cotton, even at a deep discount. Once again, local business leaders turned to Zhang for help. Together with the magistrate of Anyang, the heads of the major middle schools in the county seat, and Zhang Tianji, the chair of the county council who until recently had been the head of the middle school from which

Zhang graduated, they devised an imaginative plan: using airplanes to transport the cotton bales to the KMT-controlled city of Zhengzhou, the railway hub 120 miles south of Anyang. The airlift was to be paid for by the cotton merchants; in return for this assistance, the merchants agreed that for every three loads of cotton, one load of students would be airlifted out of the besieged city.

Back in Nanjing, Zhang used his connections to secure government permission and then approached General Claire Lee Chennault, the legendary founder and commander of the Flying Tigers, the American volunteer airmen who came to China during World War II to help fight the Japanese. Chennault had recently founded Civil Air Transport Inc. (CAT) in hopes of engaging in the civil aviation market in postwar China. The two sides quickly reached an agreement. Starting in January 1947, Civil Air Transport began airlifting cotton and students out of Anyang. The operation lasted three months, and by its end, over 5,000 young students were brought to Zhengzhou. Many of the airlifted students eventually joined the KMT evacuation to Taiwan, making Anyang one of the most represented mainland counties on the island in the following decades.

Back in Anyang, the siege lasted two more years, until the spring of 1949. Anyang's defense was solid, with the forces defending it comprised largely of former bandits who had accumulated numerous feuds with the CCP over the previous decades and were determined to fight to the end. In April of that year, Communist forces crossed the Yangtze River and "liberated" the KMT capital, Nanjing. It was clear that the KMT's cause was lost. In May, the final attack on Anyang began, led by the field army of General Lin Biao, who had been a classmate of Ma and Guo about 20 years earlier in the military academy. When the city wall was breached, Guo Qing, the commander of the city's defense and a former bandit leader, committed suicide. Zhao Zhichen, Zhang's former natural history teacher at his middle school and the regional minister, was also inside the city. He was captured and quickly executed. The last county magistrate, Huang Boying, who was the former head of the KMT's Youth League and Zhang's sworn brother, was captured and executed as well. Prior to these events, Wang Zhiquan, the bandit-turned-general of the KMT, had resigned his position, abandoned his troops and base, and self-exiled to Wuhan. However, one of his personal foes followed him there and shot him on the street.

Zhang's memoir does not specify when he left the mainland, but it must have been very late. In the last days of September 1949, just a few days before Mao ascended the Tiananmen Tower to proclaim the founding of the People's Republic of China, Zhang was still in Guangzhou, which had become the temporary capital of the KMT after the fall of Nanjing. While there, he ran into Wen Liangru, his former Chinese teacher at middle school and the Anyang County magistrate who had hired him as a communication assistant in 1925. Wen had been involved in politics in his home province of Shaanxi since then and was an unwavering anti-Communist. When Zhang asked Wen about his plans, his former teacher replied that he still needed to return to Shaanxi for some official business. They parted ways there. Two weeks later, Guangzhou fell to the Communists. Much later, Zhang learned that Wen never got the chance to leave the mainland; he was captured by the Communists and executed.

The last major KMT holdout on the mainland, the southwestern metropolis of Chengdu, fell to the Communists in December 1949. Chiang Kai-shek's airplane left Chengdu when Communist troops had already occupied part of the city. The Communist takeover of the country was soon completed. However, Chiang and the KMT managed to carry the institutional "temples" of the Republic of China to Taiwan, where they would survive, thrive, and transform for decades to come. The airlifted students and other sojourners from Anyang carried with them all the symbols of their native place and their attachment to it as they sought refuge on the island. Their only hope was to reclaim the lost country, as Chiang had pledged to lead them to. In their decades-long waiting and yearning, the "culture of locality" that had been terminated in their mainland home found renewed life.

Epilogue

1

In July 2024, I met Mr. Zhang Runshu at a coffee shop near the intersection of Xinyi Road and Yongkang Street, one of the most visited and bustling areas in the Zhongzheng District of Taipei. At 86, he looked youthful and energetic. I had tried to arrange the meeting closer to his home in the Xindian District, where Chengchi University is located, but he insisted on meeting here. He explained that this area was where his family first settled in Taipei and where he spent much of his teenage years.

We chatted for two hours about his father, Zhang Jinjian, the extended family his father brought to Taiwan in 1949, the Anyang sojourners community, and their trips back to Anyang in recent decades. After the interview, as I escorted him to the Dongmen subway station, just a two-minute walk from the coffee shop, he told me that when they first arrived in 1949, the area had been mostly rice paddies.

Mr. Zhang had retired over a decade earlier from Chengchi University, where he had served as a professor and dean of the law school. Chengchi University, formerly known as the KMT Central Political Academy, was where his father enrolled as a student in 1927 and spent most of his teaching career as a professor.

Despite attending the best high school in Taiwan, the younger Zhang chose Chengchi University over the more prestigious National Taiwan University for his college education, majoring in administrative studies—his father's specialty. Clearly, a family tradition was developing among the Zhangs in Taiwan. With both his grandfather and father buried in Taiwan, Mr. Zhang noted that the family is now five generations deep on the island, as his grandchildren have all grown up there.

Mr. Zhang's family stands out among the Anyang sojourners, as his father was the most senior of the Anyang natives to make it to Taiwan and managed to bring his own parents along. Most families can trace three, at most four, generations in Taiwan. However, the Zhang family's situation still reflects a broader trend among the Anyang natives who resettled in Taiwan in 1949. While the first generation remained deeply connected to their native place and spent decades as Anyang sojourners, their descendants inevitably became localized as natives of Taiwan.

Sojourning communities are not a new phenomenon in China, nor is the trend of sojourners' descendants taking root in their host places and becoming local natives. The high level of geographical mobility over the last three centuries of late imperial China created numerous sojourning communities within the vast country, most of which eventually localized into their new places. However, these historical sojourners maintained continuous connections with their home places and made regular trips back, where life continued to evolve according to familiar social and moral norms.

The experience of the Anyang sojourners in Taiwan, along with other sojourners from mainland China who settled on the island in 1949, marked a novel development that earlier sojourners could not have imagined: their home places had ceased to exist as they once knew them. Their longing to return became purely nostalgic, with no communication with or replenishing of new members from their home place. The struggles of these individuals—more than a million of them—in their exodus from the mainland, the anxious waiting for the recovery of the lost homeland and the painful realization of its impossibility, the endless homecomings in the imagination, and eventually the profound disappointment upon physically returning to a changed place, constitute the last chapter of this saga about the death of hometown.

2

The approximately 5,000 students airlifted out of the besieged Anyang County seat came from various private and public middle schools, high schools, and normal colleges in the county. These students were mostly teenagers, with some of their teachers accompanying them. Upon landing in Zhengzhou in central Henan, the local KMT government managed to find temporary accommodations for them and maintained the original institutional frameworks. Consequently, teachers and students continued their usual instruction and learning until central Henan fell to the Communists a year later. They then trekked farther south, either on foot or riding atop crowded cargo trains, seeking refuge in government-controlled areas. The preservation of institutional frameworks likely helped local and central government relief agencies provide assistance as they moved.

By late spring of 1949, when CCP forces breached the Yangtze River defenses and took over the KMT capital Nanjing, government support ceased. Schools dismissed their students in various locations—Zhang Jinjian's alma maters, the Anyang Middle School in Zhangshu town of Jiangxi, and the Anyang High School in Hengyang of Hunan—and ceased to exist.

Many of these students joined the KMT military on-site. With its best troops having been decimated in major military campaigns over the previous year or two, the KMT desperately needed to replenish its ranks, and the young students were ideal candidates. As the government retreated to Taiwan, a substantial number of Anyang youth followed as new military recruits. These educated young men were considered the brightest of the local society back home. Once the turmoil of the exodus subsided, they generally adapted well to their new environment in Taiwan and managed to thrive, despite enduring hardship and delayed gratification. A few examples can help illustrate their life trajectories:

- Du Dehe, born in 1931 and a student at a Catholic middle school, was 16 years old when he was airlifted out of Anyang. He joined the military, trained in Taiwan, and spent several years in service. After demobilization, he attended a foreign language school and spent most of his career as a manager in Taiwan's civil aviation industry.
- Tian Fengtai, born in 1930 and a student at the public Anyang High School, was 17 years old when he was airlifted out of Anyang. He served in the military for 20 years and was demobilized in 1969. He got married in 1972 and earned a doctoral degree from Chengchi University in 1979.

- Zhang Mingwen, born in 1929 and airlifted out of Anyang at 18 years old, was the most successful among those who joined the military. As a young officer, Mingwen excelled and received several medals and honors, but he continued to pursue his interrupted education by reading extensively. In 1961, he was finally admitted to the physics department of a college and began his academic career. He formally demobilized from the military and started working at a research institute in 1965. Zhang earned his PhD in optics from the University of Arizona in 1975. Upon returning to Taiwan, he became a leading scientist in the field of optics and soon gained international recognition for his work.

Some students returned home when they found no other options. Others took a different route, forming temporary joint schools with students from other displaced schools and trekking southward all the way to Vietnam. Several years later, they were retrieved by the KMT government and arrived in Taiwan. Duan Qingxin, born in 1928 and a student at Anyang Normal College, was among these students. She was one of the few female students airlifted out of Anyang and exiled to Vietnam at the end of the civil war. In Taiwan, she married a fellow Anyang native, completed her college education, and worked as a schoolteacher until her retirement.

The students Zhang Jinjian helped airlift out of Anyang undoubtedly constituted the largest portion of the Anyang sojourners community in Taiwan. However, there were others as well. Military personnel who joined the KMT military earlier and through other channels formed another significant segment of the community. Here are a few examples:

- Chang Xiaode, born in 1907 and a classmate of Zhang Jinjian at Anyang Middle School, enrolled in the KMT military academy in the same year as Guo Shengyong and Ma Zai. After the split between the two parties, he aligned with the Nationalists and became an officer in the KMT military. Throughout decades of warfare—first against the CCP, then against the Japanese, and finally against the CCP again—Chang was promoted to the rank of brigadier general and lost a leg in a battle. He followed the government to Taiwan and worked in the Ministry of Defense until his retirement.
- Qiao Pei, born in 1918 and a graduate of the normal college in town in 1937, was working as an elementary school teacher in Anyang when the Japanese invaded. He left his teaching position to join the KMT military and was selected for music training to support the resistance. As a music specialist in the military, he moved to Taiwan with the government and served in the air force for nearly 20 years until his retirement in 1968. After retiring, he became a music teacher and freelance writer.
- Gao Anzhe, born in 1925 in the same village as Zhang Jinjian, attended the elementary school Zhang established in 1928 on the site of the local earth temple. In 1947, while Gao was working as an apprentice in a medicine shop in the county seat, he was conscripted by the military, along with several thousand other young men from the county. Gao excelled in the military, received promotions, and followed the retreating KMT troops to Taiwan. He retired from the military at the rank of major and later enrolled at Taiwan Normal University as a literature major.

Given the authoritarian nature of the KMT regime at the time of its retreat to Taiwan, it is not surprising that the military comprised the largest portion of the personnel it brought along. However, there were also civil servants, such as Zhang Jinjian, though they were fewer in number. Amid the chaos of 1949, these individuals—men of various ages and a smaller number of women—originating from Anyang County and taking many different paths, ended up on the small island of Taiwan. Except for some students who traveled together, most did not know about each other or the presence of so many fellow Anyang natives in Taiwan. For instance, Zhang Jinjian and Chang Xiaode, two middle school classmates, had not seen or contacted each other for more than 20 years since their graduation in 1925. As the initial upheaval subsided and they began to adapt to their new circumstances, they gradually discovered each other's presence in Taiwan and, over time, started to build a community based on their common origin from Anyang.

3.

During their first decade in Taiwan, the sojourning Anyang natives spent their time preparing for an imminent reconquest of their lost homeland, much like other displaced mainlanders. They had not come to the island by choice. So they were willing to believe Chiang Kai-shek's promise that they would soon attack the mainland and reclaim their homes. In this context, Taiwan was seen merely as a temporary resting place and a launchpad for the reconquest. There was no room for nostalgia, as there was no need for it yet.

That mentality abruptly ended in October 1958 when Chiang Kai-shek, under pressure from the US government to avoid unexpected military conflicts in the Taiwan Strait, announced that the KMT would abandon its plan for military reconquest and instead resort to political means to reclaim the mainland. Confused yet perhaps also relieved, people quickly shifted their focus to settling in Taiwan, which now seemed likely to be their long-term home. Native-place associations, which had existed since 1949 to provide mutual support among mainlanders from the same region, began to flourish. In the 1960s, a new genre of publication—the "local reference" magazines—emerged, offering a space for displaced mainlanders to share, learn about, and celebrate the history, geography, and culture of their native places. For these displaced mainlanders, this marked the beginning of decades of cultural nostalgia—the yearning for an unreachable ancestral home place.

The Anyang sojourners' formal and intensive expression of nostalgia for their native county emerged a bit later, in the 1980s. Several factors likely contributed to this delay. First, the largest group of Anyang natives—the airlifted students—were mostly born around 1930. By the time the dream of a quick return home was shattered, they had just reached their thirties. Marriage, family, education, and career development all had to begin simultaneously. The practical demands of life left little room for sentimentality. It was not until they had established themselves in Taiwan that they could start to reflect on and celebrate the ancestral home they had left behind decades earlier.

Second, for those who did feel the yearning to reconnect with their native place, there was an alternative venue: the *Henan*

Reference, a "local reference" magazine founded in 1969 that focused on Henan Province. Traditionally, the literati's localist orientation operated within a nested hierarchy of local places, each corresponding to an administrative division, such as a province, prefecture, or county. These divisions could be transformed into the literati's "home places" through localist activities like writing local gazetteers or engaging in local public affairs. For example, Cui Xian and Ma Piyao could identify themselves as natives of Henan (the province), Zhangde (the prefecture), or Anyang (the county). Largely the same can be said of Zhang Jinjian, though in Zhang's case the prefecture was abolished as an entity. Thus, the more senior Anyang sojourners in Taiwan found solace for their homesickness in this provincial venue. Indeed, Zhang Jinjian was part of the leadership team of the *Henan Reference* magazine.

By the early 1980s, even the cohort of airlifted students among the Anyang sojourners had reached their fifties, and the situation had changed significantly. The yearning for the native soil from which they had been separated for three decades, along with the eagerness to talk about it, had become palpable—sometimes even unstoppable. Qiao Pei, the retired military music specialist, spent the New Year's season of 1978 scouring every bookstore in Taipei in search of an Anyang County gazetteer. He eventually found a copy of the 1820 edition, only to be enraged when he discovered that the publisher had mistakenly included a wrong city map for the Anyang County seat. He immediately went to the publisher, demanded and received an apology, and then dedicated the next year and a half to searching for the correct map in libraries and archives across Taiwan.

During their more than 30 years in Taiwan, a network of Anyang natives had gradually formed, with two notable hubs. One was Zhang Jinjian, who had earned widespread respect as the "big family head" (da jiazhang) for his generosity in helping fellow natives. The other was Duan Qingxin, the former student who had trekked to Vietnam before arriving in Taiwan and later became a schoolteacher. Duan's love of painting and her amiable personality had made her a popular artist among the Anyang sojourners. By this time, the conditions for a community of nostalgia among the sojourners had fully matured.

4

The event that directly led to the formation of a conscious community among the Anyang sojourners occurred in 1982, once again revolving around the Anyang County gazetteer. On the Dragon Boat Day (in May), two younger Anyang natives, Gao Anze and Du Dehe, both in their fifties, visited Zhang Jinjian, bringing rice dumplings as traditional gifts. They had been toying with the idea of reproducing copies of the Anyang County gazetteer, as it had long been out of stock in Taiwan despite a clear demand among the Anyang sojourners. Part of their visit's purpose was to seek advice from the respected patriarch on this matter. To their amazement, during their conversation, Zhang produced copies of the two most recent editions of the gazetteer—from 1820 and 1933. These copies were part of Zhang's personal collection, and having both versions in Taiwan was certainly a rarity.

On the very same day, Gao and Du visited a publisher to inquire about the details and costs of reprinting the two gazetteers together. A few days later, another meeting took place in Zhang's study, bringing together several other Anyang natives, including Duan the painter and Zhang's son, Runshu. During this meeting, a plan was finalized: they would begin the reprinting process while simultaneously collecting and creating an address list of Anyang sojourners in Taiwan. The initial funds were donated by Zhang Jinjian and those present, with the remaining costs to be covered by selling the gazetteers to fellow Anyang sojourners at cost price. An additional decision was made: once completed, the address list of Anyang sojourners would be included as an appendix in the reprinted gazetteer.

The address list appended to the reprinted gazetteer featured 333 names, marking the first formal recognition of the Anyang sojourners community. In the following years, the list was adjusted as more names were discovered, eventually reaching about 400 families at its peak, according to the recollections of community elders. The small group responsible for the reprint, led by Zhang Jinjian, began referring to themselves as the "Editing Board of *Anyang References*," mirroring the common practice among mainlander sojourners of publishing "local reference" magazines—though at that time, an Anyang-focused magazine had yet to exist. This changed in 1985 when the *Anyang References* magazine was founded and began publishing annually. In addition to historical and geographic knowledge of the region, the magazine featured memoirs recounting the sojourners' early experiences in Anyang and their journeys to Taiwan, as well as articles on local customs, shrines, festivals, fairs, and folklore drawn from their memories. The magazine continued for 33 years until its closure in 2018, by which time the first generation of Anyang sojourners had largely passed away, and the second generation lacked an interest in continuing the legacy.

The *Anyang References* magazine was quintessentially a publication of nostalgia, deeply immersed in the yearning for a distant place and a bygone era. While the reprinted gazetteer helped the sojourners imagine their unreachable homeland, the magazine took it a step further by enabling them to actively, albeit vicariously, reconstruct their native place through personal reminiscences. The magazine's purpose was made explicit in the opening statement of its first issue, where the editing board positioned the magazine as a substitute for the renewal of the county gazetteer. "Since the home place has fallen, and we are exiles on this island," the statement read, "no one is presiding over the affairs of the county, and a formal renewal of the gazetteer is now impossible […] yet we can never give up this noble goal." The magazine, therefore, was seen as a way to "prepare for and contribute to the future project of the county gazetteer's formal compilation." To further reinforce their identity as the true preservers of a lost homeland, the sojourners even created an Anyang County anthem, with lyrics penned by Zhang Jinjian and music composed by Qiao Pei (Figure 11).

During the first two decades, the team responsible for editing the *Anyang References* magazine also organized an annual community banquet during the traditional Chinese New Year season. The banquet was always held at a restaurant in Taipei, drawing Anyang natives from across the island. As proposed by Zhang Jinjian, each banquet began with a special ritual: an offering to the native place ancestors. A tablet, inscribed with "the spirit of all the ancestors of Anyang County of Henan Province (河南省安陽縣列祖列宗之神位)" was placed at the center of the banquet hall. Led by a "chief priest (主祭)," the attendees offered flowers,

Figure 11 The Anthem of Anyang County (Source: *Anyang References*, volume 2, p. 1)

burned incense, and bowed three times toward the tablet. In the early years, Zhang Jinjian served as the chief priest. After his death in 1988, the role was filled by one of the community's most revered members, chosen on the spot by the gathering.

The idea of the ancestral ritual at the community banquet aligns closely with the ethos behind reprinting the county gazetteer. As Zhang Jinjian stated in the preface of the reprinted gazetteer, its purpose was to fulfill the sojourners' "yearning for returning to the native soil and participating in the ancestral rituals." These ancestral rituals, traditionally conducted by individual clans or families in their ancestral place, could not be performed in the conventional manner due to their physical separation from the native land. In response, the sojourners in Taiwan created a novel ritual that united the ancestors of different clans into a collective "ancestors of Anyang."

In the late imperial period, ancestral rituals and lineage construction activities played a crucial role in bringing together the processes of local identity formation and kinship identity formation, thereby binding the literati to their local place. However, in the unique modern context of sojourning in Taiwan, we witness a distinct scenario where ancestral gods have completely merged into a territorial deity, resulting in a convergence of local and kinship identities.

If we agree that home is a place to dwell, live, and die, then in Zhang Jinjian's imagination, Anyang became the ultimate dwelling place in the truest sense. In this vision, Anyang completely transcended its role as an administrative entity and transformed into a place where one joins their kinsfolk and ancestors. Yu Ying-shih, a distinguished modern historian of literati culture, described the "native place" as "the place where, in old times, the literati would return at the end of their careers, choosing it as the place to die and be buried." The rituals performed by Zhang Jinjian and the Anyang sojourners rendered Anyang precisely as such a place. It is perhaps only in this human-place relationship that Heidegger's ideal of a dwelling place can fully resonate: "accepting the heavens, preserving the earth, awaiting the divine, and accompanying the moral."

Yet, this idealized vision existed only in the imagination. The sojourners were physically separated from their homeland. They did not have even a detailed map of it. In 1988, the first year the KMT government in Taiwan lifted its travel ban to the mainland, a pioneering traveler brought back an atlas of Anyang County, which included detailed maps of each of the ten districts. When this atlas was presented at the following New Year's banquet, it caused a sensation among the sojourners. People gathered around it, eagerly studying the roads and trails they once knew, and the villages they had lived in or visited.

In response to this overwhelming thirst for connection to their native soil, the editorial board decided to reprint the atlas. This decision was meant both to satisfy the sojourners' longing and to assist them in their future homecoming trips. This moment of intense yearning for their native place was likely the peak of their decades-long nostalgia. Soon they would confront the reality on the ground and face disillusionment when they physically returned to their homeland.

5

The travel bans on people living in "free China" to visit the "fallen area" of the mainland were lifted in late 1987 by Chiang Kai-shek's son, Chiang Ching-kuo. This lifting of the ban resulted from the pressures of the Veteran Homecoming Movement, which was launched by mainlanders who retreated to the island with the KMT and in cooperation with the newly arising opposition party, the Democratic Progressive Party. By then, Taiwan had not only gone through more than two decades of rapid economic growth and become one of the "newly industrialized economies," but it had also entered a stage of liberalization and democratization. The martial law that had been imposed since 1949 and restricted free media and alternative political parties was finally lifted. Taiwan was steadily on its way to becoming a prosperous and open society.

Hundreds of thousands of retired military personnel and civil servants who had been waiting for this moment flooded to the mainland over the following years. When they finally set foot in the places they had been obsessed with for decades, most were profoundly disappointed and even traumatized. Despite the sojourners' long-held wish to return, few actually resettled on the mainland when it eventually became possible. The main reason for this, as recent studies have shown, is that their native places had changed beyond recognition for the returning sojourners, who found themselves to be outsiders in their homeland. A real sense of homelessness, rather than the yearning for a home they could not return to, emerged from these homecoming journeys and tragically ended the decades-long painful but sweet yearning.

The homecoming trips of the Anyang natives largely confirm this picture. However, the accounts of these trips published in the *Anyang Reference* magazine also make it clear that the changes their native place underwent during the previous four decades were comprehensive, encompassing ecology, economy, landscape, and urban layout, as well as the mental and spiritual state of the people. What they saw in Anyang was almost incompatible with their memories of the place they had left behind and their current lives in Taiwan. The hometown had long since died; they just did not realize it until now.

Zhao Chao made his first trip in 1989 when he was 69 years old. The first things he saw in his hometown were disappointing: when he disembarked the train at the Anyang Railway Station, he could still recognize that the luggage house was the same as it had been 40 years before, but the two huge, simplified characters "An-yang" displayed atop the station building were "so tasteless." The city wall, which held many fond childhood memories for him, was gone. These two changes were the most conspicuous ones that disturbed Zhao. In fact, the simplification of the Chinese characters and the demolition of the city walls were among the most permanent visual impacts the CCP imposed on China after their takeover. Everywhere the Chinese written words, which used to be the most concrete sign of Chinese civilization and the foundation of its sense of superiority, were replaced by something simpler and supposedly easier for the masses to learn, but also uglier in the eyes of the educated. Almost everywhere, city walls were demolished, erasing the most common landscape feature of traditional civilization to make more room for urban growth. Zhao understood that underlying these changes was the logic of a country of the "working class," toward which he had never concealed his disdain.

More disturbing was the culture of the working-class country. Almost all sites of historical significance within the city, such as the tallest Buddhist pagoda and the retreat of Han Qi, the Sung dynasty prime minister, were closed to the public and required personal connections for access. Meetings are too frequent, and some of the terms related to meetings, such as "taolun (discussion)" are discomforting. Service personnel were cold and rude to customers. However, public attitudes toward the party leaders followed a pattern of gratitude and praise. All these common features of a totalitarian society filled Zhao with contempt. One corner of the city wall had been recently restored, and a stele was erected on-site, with inscriptions praising the local CCP leaders for making the restoration possible. The flattering tone of the inscription made Zhao angry, given how much the "leaders" had ruined the world he held dear. What Zhao did not know was that the author of the stele inscription, who had devoted himself to writing a sequel to the literary classic *Dreams of the Red Chamber*, was one of the rare independent-minded scholars in Anyang. His praises of the local party leader were most likely just following the formula of commemorative essays in the PRC, part of the invisible social norm necessary for anyone to survive.

Hu Shengtang was much younger. Born in 1932, he was only 15 when he was airlifted out of the county seat. As the oldest son of his parents, he felt particularly guilty for not being able to fulfill his filial duty. So, when the travel ban was lifted, he persevered through petitions for early retirement from his teaching position at a military academy and prepared for his dream trip.

The political turmoil of 1989, when a pro-democratic movement in Beijing was cracked down on with a bloodbath, delayed the trip. However, as soon as the situation stabilized, he set off in the spring of 1990.

Hu's flight brought him to Zhengzhou. Unwilling to wait another day for a train ticket, he hired a taxi for the 120-mile journey between Zhengzhou and Anyang. When the taxi broke down on the road, the driver attempted to hail another vehicle to continue the trip. Hu witnessed firsthand people's indifference to the troubles of others; none of the passing drivers even slowed down. Fortunately, they were able to catch a long-distance bus on the Zhengzhou-Anyang route. Onboard, Hu eagerly greeted the passengers, most of whom were fellow natives of Anyang. However, he was met with a sea of emotionless faces. The basic decency and politeness Hu had become accustomed to during his 40 years in Taiwan had long since become an oddity in Anyang—a fact I can confirm from my own experience growing up there during the Communist era.

By temperament, Hu was optimistic and warmhearted. He never hid his pride at being promoted to the rank of brigadier general at the military academy and was always eager to help friends and relatives. After several attempts by Hu, a young passenger on the bus began to respond to his greetings and told him he envied the wealthy lifestyle of people in Taiwan. When the bus arrived at the Anyang bus station, Hu was extorted for a small fortune by a tricycle driver who charged him 20 RMB to pull his luggage for just a few hundred yards. In 1990, 100 RMB a month was considered a decent salary for most people in Anyang. Hu hired another taxi to take him to his home village, about six miles from the station, for 45 RMB. Such price gouging made Hu a bit unhappy, but he brushed it aside and rushed home. The villages were dilapidated, and the crop fields looked dry and lifeless. Again, this was a bit disappointing, but there was no time to be bothered by it.

He finally got home, saw all the relatives, and knelt down in front of his aged mother to apologize for his unfulfilled duties all these years. He was surprised to hear relatives telling him that they were much satisfied with life now that they had enough to eat. Through correspondence beforehand, he had learned that his father was "struggled to death" during the land reform in the home village, shortly after he left Anyang. The next day he asked one of his brothers to lead him to their father's tomb. They carried incense and tomb sacrifices for an offering. But at the tomb site, they found no tomb. His brother told him the tomb had long since been erased by the people's commune—the unit of collectivized agriculture under Mao—to make more space for farming. So, they burned incense and made offering at the approximate place where his father used to be buried.

Hu admitted that his feelings about the homecoming journey were mixed. Despite the unpleasant details and moments of disappointment, he enjoyed the reunions with family members and relatives. He made several trips back, mainly because his mother was still in the village. However, resettling there was out of the question. The imagined native soil, where one could rest with ancestors—as the ancient local worthies had preached and practiced—was simply impossible anymore. He could not even locate his father's resting place. At the end of one trip, when he arrived home in Taipei late at night, he felt so relieved to be finally home.

Both Zhao and Hu were relatively lucky, as their relatives in Anyang did not make it too hard for them. Numerous accounts of homecoming trips by natives of Anyang and elsewhere show that relatives in their native places, ravaged by decades of terror, poverty, and abuse of power, could become petty and disgraceful, continually asking the returning sojourners for financial support to the visitors' breaking point. Many were traumatized by this. Yet, even for those who were spared such trauma, their homecoming journeys were enough to shatter their dreams of their native soil and homeland. In reality, it simply does not exist anymore.

Zhang Jinjian never made it back. Had he done so, there would have been much embarrassment waiting for him in Anyang. Once the most famous native of Anyang, he was simply erased from the collective memory, partly because of his political affiliation. Even the collection of oral history sources created by the local government in the 1980s and 1990s—mostly based on the memories of people who had experienced recent historical events—did not mention him at all. Ma Zai was still remembered by some of the locals, but even the memory of Ma was quickly fading away. A serious believer in the Communist cause—indeed, a serious believer in any cause—was an oddity in the post-Mao era. The new focal point was whoever was in power, like the local party leaders praised in the stele at the corner of the restored city wall. People didn't even need to remember what their names were. They just needed to follow the formula, give praise, and expect rewards for playing the game. Even if granted a chance to return and resettle, it is hard to imagine that such a place would be what Zhang would want, or for that matter what

Han Qi of the Song dynasty, Cui Xian of the Ming, or Ma Piyao of the Qing would have desired. To use Heidegger's metaphor, it became a place where gods have fled.[21]

Discussion Questions

1. What are the most important factors that could lead to the natives of a place losing connection with it?
2. Why do people need local roots? Or do they? If they do, what are the possible ways to take root in a local place?
3. Write an essay discussing the relationship between people and the place in your hometown or home state.

Notes

1. Martin Heidegger, *Vorträge und Aufsätze* (Stuttgart: Klett-Cotta, 2004), 158–159，188–189.

2. Robert Hymes, Introduction to Robert Hymes and Konrad Schirokauer, eds., *Ordering the World Approaches to State and Society in Sung Dynasty China* (Berkeley: University of California Press, 1993): 4.

3. Ray Huang, *1587, A Year of No Significance: The Ming Dynasty in Decline* (New Haven: Yale University Press, 1982).

4. Cui Xian, *Huanci, Juan 7*.

5. Cited by Yu Ying-shih, "The Radicalization of China in the Twentieth Century," *Daedalus* (Spring 1993), 137.

6. Henriette Harrison, *Man Awakened from Dreams: One Man's Life in a North China Village, 1857–1942* (Stanford: Stanford University Press, 2005).

7. Deyiyongren 得一庸人, "Concise Report on My Overseas Experiences 海外見聞錄", in *Wanguo Gongbao* 萬國公報, Oct. 1889.

8. See Leo Lee, *Shanghai Modern* (Cambridge, MA: Harvard University Press, 1999), for the issue of mimicry and its absence in Chinese context.

9. Fairbank, *The Chinese World Order* (Cambridge, MA: Harvard University Press, 1973), 1–2, for a recent discussion of the "all-under-heaven" concept. See also Wang Ban, ed., *Chinese Visions of World Order: Tianxia, Culture, and World Politics* (Durham, NC: Duke University Press, 2017).

10. Wang Yangming, "Gaoping xian zhi xu 高平縣志序", in *Wang wencheng quanshu* 王文成全書 (Electronic Siku quanshu edition), juan 29.

11. Yongtao Du, "Locality and Local Gazetteers from the Qing to the Republic: A Case for Continuity in Spatial Order," *Journal of Chinese History* (2023), 7, 125–155.

12. Cheng Renqing 程任卿, *Sijuan quanshu* 絲絹全書 (*Siku quanshu Cunmu congshu* edition), 8:8a.

13. Zhang Jinjian, *Junquan zhuyi yu defang zhidu* 均權主義與地方制度 (Zhengzhong shuju, 1948), 1–7.

14. Lenin, V. What Is to Be done? In Selected Works of V. Lenin (Moscow: Foreign Languages Publishing House, 1961), 347–530. Here, chapter 3.3: "Political Exposures and 'Training in Revolutionary Activity.'"

15. See Hans J. Van de Ven, *From Friend to Comrade: The Founding of the Chinese Communist Party, 1920–1927* (Berkeley: University of California Press, 1991). Also Michael Y. L. Luk, *The Origins of Chinese Bolshevism: An Ideology in the Making, 1920–1928* (Hong Kong; New York: Oxford University Press, 1990), 216. Luk called this wave of thought reform the first "rectification."

16. Liu Shaoqi, *How to be a Good Communist*, Liu Shaoqi Reference Archive, Chapter 6, https://www.marxists.org/reference/archive/liu-shaoqi/1939/how-to-be/index.htm.

17. The event was reported in *US Survey of the China Mainland Press* (no. 1850, September 10, 1958, p. 24). Cited by David S. G. Goodman, "Structuring Local Identity: Nation, Province and County in Shanxi during the 1990s," *China Quarterly* 172 (December 2002): 837.

18. Mao Zedong, "Serve the People," in *Selected Works of Mao Zedong* (CITY: Foreign Languages Press, 1965) vol. 3. Emphasis added. The traditional way of including one's place of origin as a standard part of one's personal information was retained in Communist China; but given the Communist anti-localist

mentality, it appears a residue of the old world, meant for the Communist cadres to overcome rather than uphold.

19. Mao, "Lun shi da guanxi," in *Mao Zedong xuanji*毛澤東選集 (Beijing: Renmin chubanshe, 1977, 267–288.
20. https://i.ifeng.com/c/8CHYyXAltDQ&wd=&eqid=e66be5970 0032f130000000264659784
21. Charles Bambach, *Heidegger's Roots: Nietzsche, National Socialism and the Greeks* (Ithaca: Cornell University Press, 2005), XXII.

Recommended Further Readings

1. Henriette Harrison, *Man Awakened from Dreams: One Man's Life in a North China Village, 1857–1942*.
2. Joseph Esherick and Mary Rankin, eds. *Chinese Local Elites and Patterns of Domination*.
3. Joseph Levenson, *Confucian China and Its Modern Fate*.

Index

Age of Division. xxi

All-under-heaven. xiv, xv, xxvii, 1, 2, 51, 53

Anarchism. 6

Antagonism. 47

Anti-banditry campaign. 13

Anti-Communist. 96

Anti-imperialist movement. 25

Anti-imperialist protests. 10

Anti-traditionalism. 6

Anyang County. xv, 4, 12, 13, 51, 52, 56, 68, 70, 96, 101, 105, 107, 108, 113

Anyang References magazine. 109, 110, 115

Apocalyptic imagery. 86

Barbarians. 33

Barbaric Conquest. ix

Bolshevization. 76, 77

Canada's Presbyterian Church. 7

Cartographic technologies. 57

Central Country. xiv

Checks and balances concept. 66

China; archaeological discovery. xi; foreign powers. 3; homelessness. xiii; human-place relationship. 71; intellectual culture. xiii, 6; kinship organization. xxi; nation-state. 2; political power. xvii, xix; proletariat nation. 47; public administration studies. 32; rural challenges. 41; self-proclaimed centrality. xv; social-moral order. xvii

China Proper. 23

China's Destiny. 48

China-based cultural reconstruction. 48

Chinese Communist Party (CCP). xvii, 25, 28, 37, 41, 43, 69, 74, 75, 76, 78, 79, 85, 86, 90, 102, 115

Chinese gentry. xix

Chinese labor movement. 10

Chinese nationalism. 2

Civic virtues. 2

Civil Air Transport Inc. (CAT). 95

Civil service examination system. xix, xxii, 3, 4, 5, 14

Class antagonism. 87
Classless society. 81
Commercial Press. 34
Communication channel. 53
Communism. xiii, 6, 11, 18, 19, 83, 87
Communist disruption. 71
Conflict. 17
Confucian society. 2
Confucianism. xvii, 48
Corruption. 16
Cosmological symbolism. 5
County gazetteer bureau. 56
Cronyism. 30
Culture of locality. 97

Doctrine of power-balance. 66
Dreams of the Red Chamber. 116

Election campaigns. 69
Elementary student readers. 60

Factionalism. 16
Feminism. 6
Fight the Communists first strategy. 41
First Sino-Japanese War. 8, 23
Franco-Prussian War. xxxi

Gazetteer project. 55, 57, 58, 65
Golden age. 9, 15

Golden Decade. 30
Government-sponsored grain storage project. xxix
Grand Harmony. 61
Great Proletarian Cultural Revolution. 76

Harmony of the people. xxxi
Henan Reference magazine. 107
Home places. 51, 56, 64, 65, 107
Home schooling. 5
Homelessness. xiii
Home-Reclaiming Regiment. 64
How to Be a Good Communist (Liu). 78
Human Nature, Party Spirit, and Individuality. 79
Huojia County. 11

Imperial system. 4
Imperialism. 23, 25, 85
Imported foreign machinery. 8
Independent effort. 43
Industrialization. 30
Internship. 29

Japanese aggression. 10

Kinship identity formation. xxii
KMT Central Political Academy. 99

Land tax collection procedures. 40

League of Loyal and Righteous Youth. 37
Liberalism. 6, 47
Lineage-building project. 21, 22
Literary culture. 6
Literati. xiv, xix, xxiii, xxiv, xxv, 14, 17, 18, 21, 51, 54, 107, 113
Literature Revolution. 26
Lithographic printing. 57
Local identity formation. xxii
Local self-governance. 53, 65, 67, 71
Localist strategies. xx
Localist strategy par excellence. xx

Magistrate's deputy. 12
Maoism. 77
Marxism-Leninism. xvii, 76, 77, 83
Massive displacement. 43
Militarist culture. 9
Military campaigns. 102
Mimicry. 34
Ming dynasty. xxii, xxiii, 21, 51, 55, 65
Mining technologies. 8
Modern education. 9, 10
Moral autonomy. xxv
My Life of Battles. 91

Nanjing regime. 28

National Academy of Social Sciences. 17
National Political Consultation Assembly. 45, 64, 68
Nationalism. xvii, 10, 44, 47, 48
Nationalist Party (KMT). xvii, xviii, 12, 18, 20, 25, 26, 27, 29, 30, 56, 60, 65, 69, 84, 93, 96, 97, 102, 103, 105, 114
Nationalist Revolution. 12, 25, 28, 59, 88
Nation-state. 2
Native place. xii, xiv, xv, xvi, 65, 94, 106, 112
Nepotism. 30
New Culture Movement. xvii, 6, 25, 26, 76
New Youth magazine. 6
Nostalgia. 106, 113

Office of Student Conduct. 38
One World Philosophy. 1
Orthodox learning. xvii, 4, 14, 16

Party activism. 25
Party-building. 77
Patriotism. 38, 39
People's Republic of China (PRC). 2
Political activism. 36
Political aspirations. 11, 17
Political culture. xxiii

Political engagement. 11
Polity crisis. 52
Principle of Democratic Centralism. 79
Principle of maximum efficiency. 66
Professional knowledge. 41
Proletariat consciousness. 74, 75, 76, 77, 78, 83
Provincial Constitution Movement. 54
Provincial-level institutions. 57
Psychological effect. xxx
Public administration. 35

Qing dynasty. xxii, xxiii, 3, 4, 5, 6, 7, 8, 14, 21, 23, 24, 48, 54, 55, 86
Quintessential localist strategy. 21

Railway construction. 24
Rectification. 77
Rectification Movement. 77, 79
Refugees. 63, 94
Revolutionary movement. 8
Roaming intellectuals. 18
Ruins of the Yin. ix, xi, xv
Rural Reconstruction Movement. 39
Russo-Japanese War. 4

Scientism. x

Second Sino-Japanese War. 30
Shang dynasty. ix
Shaoshan Revisited. 82
Sino-centric world. xv
Sng dynasty. xxii
Social transformation. 29
Socialism. 6
Sojourning communities. 100, 103
Song dynasty. 120
Spiritual crisis. xiii
Student-army. 88
Subjectivity loss. 34
Sung dynasty. xxvi, 116

Ta Kung Pao newspaper. 58
The New People. 2
Traditional Chinese civilization. xv, xxx, 92, 115
Traditional Chinese society. 51
Tunnel warfare. 90
Tutelary rule. 67

Unbound Foot Society. 10
Uncertainty. 15
Universalism. 80

Veteran Homecoming Movement. 114

Warlord politics. 10

Warlordism. 6, 85

Wedding ceremony. 19

Western culture. 1

Working-class consciousness. 74

Working-class country. 116

Wuhan regime. 28

Xenophobia. 3

Xia dynasty. xi

Xinxiang County. 12

Youth league. 39

Zhangde Prefecture. xxv, 52

www.ingramcontent.com/pod-product-compliance
Lightning Source LLC
Chambersburg PA
CBHW070808230426
43665CB00017B/2528